Published by Instigator Press
1330 20th Street
San Francisco, California, USA
+1.650.618.9553

Book Design: Michael Braley
Photography: Chris Conroy,
Gilles Frydman, Victor Penner,
Lily Piel, Sarah Thorpe
Copy Editor: Darcy Kendall,
Kristen Pinheiro
Index: Maria Sosnowski
Printed in Canada by Blanchette Press

Names: Bielenberg, John, author | Burn, Mike,
author | Dickinson, Elizabeth Evitts, author |
Galle, Greg, author.

Title: Think wrong: how to conquer the
status quo and do work that matters / by
John Bielenberg, Mike Burn, Greg Galle,
and Elizabeth Evitts Dickinson.

Description: Instigator paperback edition. |
San Francisco : Instigator Press, 2016

Identifiers: LCCN 2016956946 (print) |
ISBN 9780692693322 (softcover) |
ISBN 9780692780688 (epub)

Subjects: Business & Economics—
Decision-Making & Problem Solving |
Business & Economics—Development—
Business Development | Business &
Economics—Entrepreneurship
LC record available at
https://lccn.loc.gov/2016956946

Think Wrong

By John Bielenberg, Mike Burn, and Greg Galle, with Elizabeth Evitts Dickinson

How to Conquer
the Status Quo
and Do Work
That Matters

Contents

T C W

Another
breakthrough
idea smacked
to the ground.

a
c
k
!

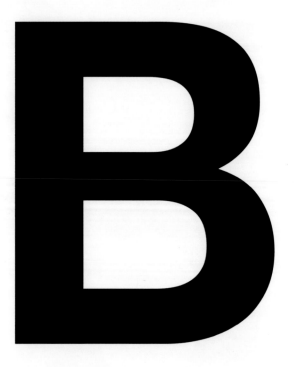

**Another bold step forward
sent sprawling back.**

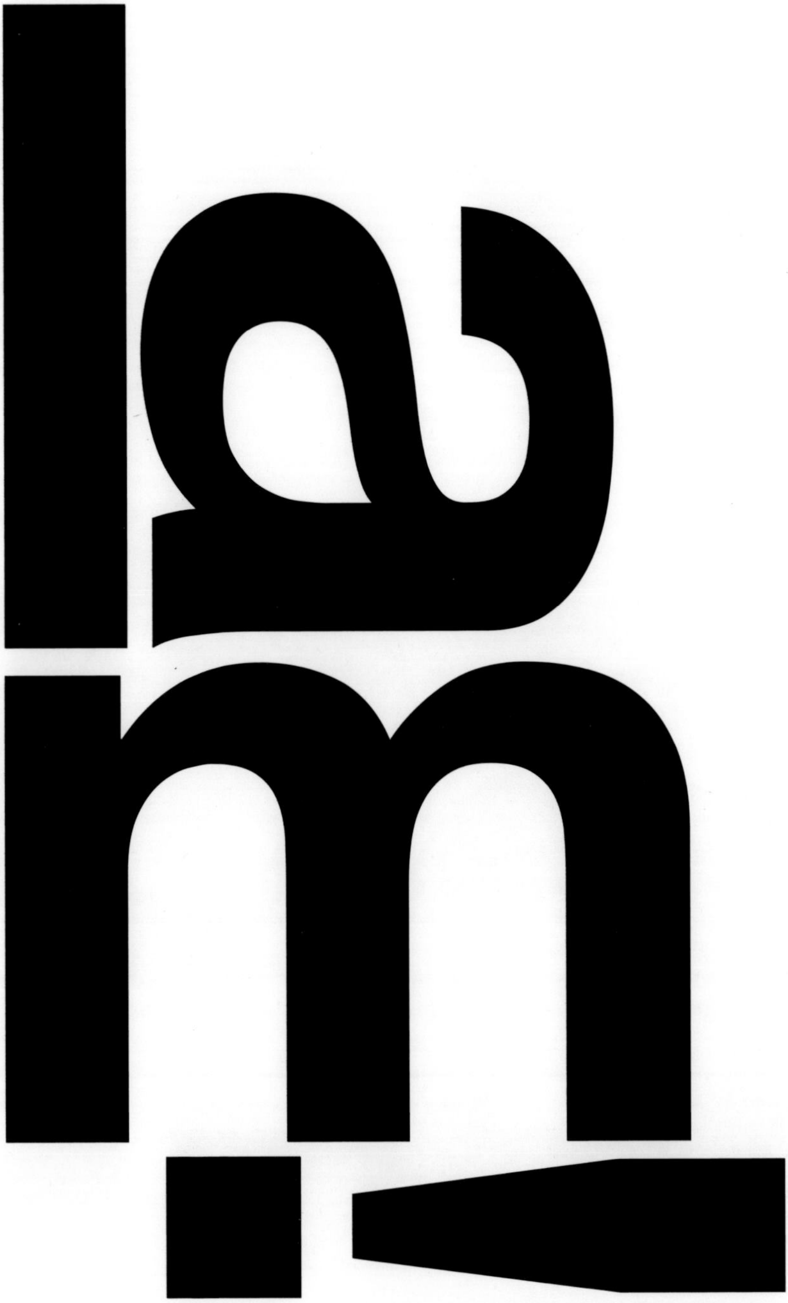

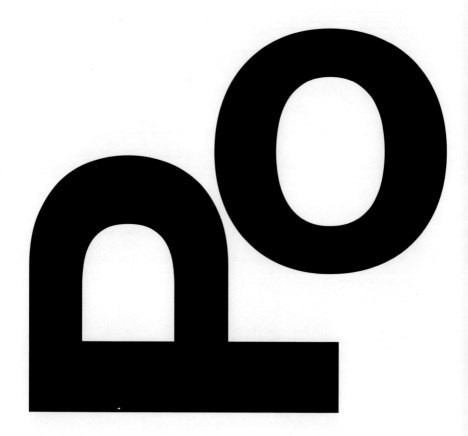

A stiff uppercut
to progress.

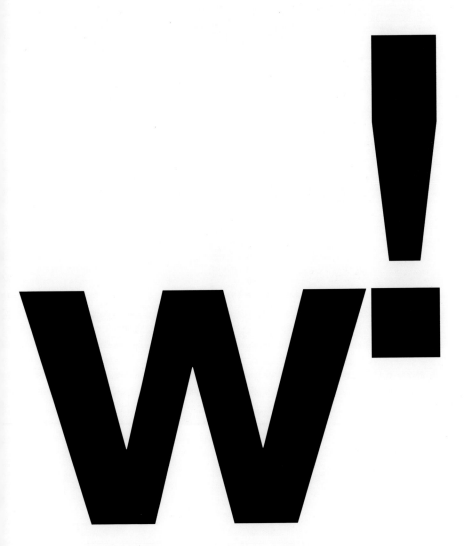

The door to a better tomorrow slams shut.

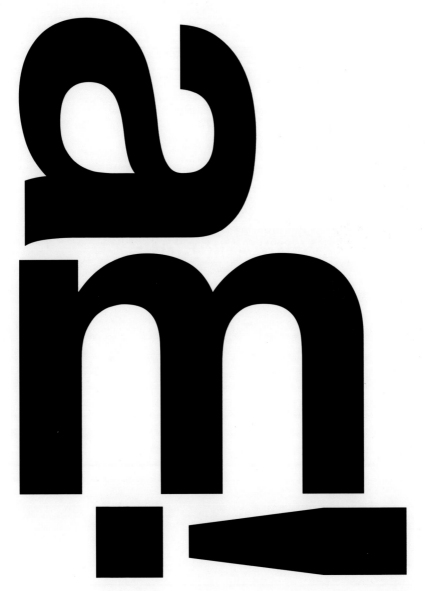

We suspect you
know how this feels.

You're excited about
something—an idea
or a new solution
with real potential.

You share the epiphany
with your boss, your
board, your colleagues,
your investors, your friends.

And this happens.

Pf
f
f

ss
st

Let me play devil's advocate.

We could never...

What
would
the
lawyers
say?

That's
nuts.

You can't
be serious.

An opportunity to do something that truly matters is extinguished, yet again.

Welcome to the club.

We're here to tell you that you're not alone.

All over the world, people just like you believe there is a
nobler, better way to work, live, and bring novel and life-
altering solutions, services, products, experiences, policies,
processes, and businesses into the world, but they are
continually derailed by the pervasive power of the status
quo. Our human default is to defend and maintain the existing state of affairs. The status quo is insidious, and it comes
in many forms. It's the weekly meeting where nothing happens. It's the rigid job description that prevents exploration.
It's the pro forma best practices peddled as the panacea
for all problems. It's the culture afraid to take risks and the
org charts that keep us from collaborating. Behavioral scientists have studied status quo bias for decades, and research
shows that the more difficult the decision, the more likely
humans will not act. Just look to the polar ice caps for a
staggering example. Time and again, humans choose the
known over the unknown.

If you're one of the ambitious ones crazy enough to
rail against the status quo—to keep bringing new ideas and
options to the fore—you likely know how it feels to be blown
off, shut down, and told you're overreaching or naïve. And
when the world continually conspires against your efforts,
you can be forgiven for losing steam. Next time, you might
even act as your own destroyer. "What if we . . . forget it.
It's going to be too hard."

Pfffssst.

So, what's
going on here?

So, what's going on here? Why are so many possibilities killed instead of kindled? Why is it so hard to bring something original and meaningful into the world?

Well, let's go back a bit.

To 1662.

To a basement laboratory inside Oxford University, to take a peek inside our heads.

A scientist named Thomas Willis had gathered a crowd to conduct what would become one of many examinations of the human brain. Willis believed the stuff inside our skull contained the secrets to our very being, and he endeavored to map the brain's inner workings. Today Willis is credited as a founder of neurology. In the 17th century, though, some considered him a madman.

Willis's theories deviated sharply from the standard assumptions of the day, which included the belief that a person's feelings and thoughts were driven by spirit, not some tangle of neurons and chemistry inside the head. Willis was "anatomizing the soul," as writer Carl Zimmer explains in his book *Soul Made Flesh,* and this idea was not at all popular, particularly with the higher-ups at the Vatican. Willis persisted against great odds and, at times, great contempt.

Look over the course of human existence, and you see flashpoints of change driven by people such as Willis who challenged the status quo. Galileo was convicted of heresy

1   2

1 Today, Thomas Willis is credited as a founder of neurology. In the 17th century, though, some considered him a madman. **2** Malala Yousafzai took a bullet for advocating the education of women in the Swat Valley of Pakistan.

for saying the sun, and not the earth, was the center of the universe. Einstein's books were burned. The Wright Brothers were considered crazy for suggesting a man might pilot a flying machine. Academia blackballed George Zweig and called him a charlatan for suggesting invisible subatomic particles formed matter. Malala Yousafzai took a bullet in the head for advocating the education of women in the Swat Valley of Pakistan.

Without these pioneering individuals and teams, we would not have the inventions and movements that changed humanity. There would be no printing press or airplane, no civil rights or Cubism, no penicillin or personal computer.

The people at the center of such advancements are the ones we remember for altering the world, for shifting the trajectory of everything that came after. In their time they were called heretics, madmen, lunatics, egotists, devils. Today we call them by different names.

We call them pioneers, masters, innovators, leaders, and heroes.

And we're here to tell you that every single one of these people, over the course of history, had one thing in common. Just one secret to their genius.

They could think wrong.

1   2

1 Pablo Picasso changed the way we look at the world. 2 Henry Bessemer used his creative naïveté to transform how things are built.

**Thinking wrong is conquering biology and culture
to change how things are to how they might be.**

Thinking wrong is how a guy named Henry Bessemer
helped usher in the Industrial Revolution. Bessemer invented
the technique for mass-producing steel in the 1800s. When
asked how he bested his competitors, the British inventor
credited one, singular advantage: "I had no fixed ideas
derived from long-established practice to control and bias
my mind, and did not suffer from the general belief that
whatever is, is right."

How many times have you thought this yourself?
Looked at a problem, at a process, at the way the world is,
and thought, *There has to be a better way.*

Well, you're right.

There is a better way.

And we're here to teach you how to do it.

We're going to show you how to think wrong so you
can triumph over the critical obstacles that emerge when
trying to turn a unique vision into reality. We're going to show
you the moments when the status quo—individuals
and systems invested in doing things as they've always
been done—rear up to kick you in the ass.

The moment when the status quo wants you to define
the problem, but you want to dream about what's possible—
daring to make a difference.

There has to
be a better way.

The moment when the status quo wants you to research best practices, but you want to find fresh inspirations— disrupting the way things might be done.

The moment when the status quo wants a single right answer, but you want to imagine as many solutions as you can—stretching beyond biases and orthodoxies to expand what's possible.

The moment when the status quo wants you to implement that single right answer, but you want to explore your most promising ideas—gaining insight that can be obtained only through making.

The moment when the status quo wants you to scale that single right answer, but you want to experiment with your most promising ideas—discovering what might work without risking it all.

The moment when the status quo wants you to defend your solution, but you want to share all you have learned— so others can help make your solution better and achieve impact sooner.

This book will give you the tools to imagine and identify the solutions that deserve to be explored and developed, as well as the framework and language to defend nascent solutions against the naysayers. We're going to teach you to move from debating to doing, and how you can continually improve and evolve your idea. Finally we'll show you how to use what you've learned to accelerate getting your solution out into the world—a solution that has real impact.

The simple truth is that our brains conspire against us.

Is it easy to think wrong? No. At least not at first. And here's why.

Today we might not stand trial for heresy as Galileo did, but we do stand trial. Every single day. We stand judged against the orthodoxy of what's acceptable. The mainstream, understood norms of how things are supposed to get done. What will work, what won't. We might be encouraged with pat phrases and told to think "outside the box" or "disrupt," but the fact is, humans loathe disruption. We love routine.

It's not all our fault. We're wired for it. The simple truth is our brains conspire against us. Today Thomas Willis would be amazed at how an MRI lights up the brain to show the neural activity inside our heads. What we've learned in the 300-plus years since Willis defended his science against detractors is that the brain is an incredibly powerful and efficient thing.

That efficiency is also our downfall.

We're born with a vast network of neurons. As we grow, we learn. Language, reasoning, motor skills. Our brains develop synaptic circuits to help us survive and become more efficient. We now know babies as young as four months old have the bandwidth to decipher and categorize events in their brains. We know that with time, our minds weigh certain information based on experience and create pathways that enable us to make quick, shortcut decisions. That's a good thing. Imagine if you had to relearn to tie your shoes each morning. Life would be chaos.

We tend to return to the familiar, well-trodden paths in our brain.

The synapses we employ most frequently develop strong connections, while the brain eliminates those we rarely tap. "Synaptic pruning" is what neuroscientists call it. By the time we reach adulthood, our brain has lopped off thousands of surplus connections.

The unintended consequence of this biological pruning is that we have a hell of a time overcoming habits. We follow the circuits formed in the brain whether we want to or not. Here's an experiment. Try talking by putting words together in a nonsensical sequence.

Hard, right?

It's difficult to speak incorrectly because our brains were so efficient at creating the synaptic connections necessary to speak properly.

And this is why we get stuck. We can say we want to change how things get done, but it's in the act of realizing that change when we stumble. That's a bad thing. Our mental efficiency mucks up our ability to problem solve. We tend to return to the familiar, well-trodden paths in our brain—what Bessemer referred to as those long-established practices that control and bias the mind.

Following the same synaptic connections, however, yields the same answer. Meanwhile, the brilliant solution you seek most likely lives outside those normal pathways.

If our first hurdle is our own mind, our second hurdle is everyone else's.

1　　　　**2**

1 Richard Dyson bucked the status quo of "Big Vacuum" and invented a better, more powerful way to suck dirt. 2 Jane Goodall lets primates in Tanzania, rather than academics at universities, inspire new insights into chimp and human behavior.

Like the brain, human society forms shortcuts. Spend 10 minutes in a middle school, and you observe all you need to of human pack mentality. Dress this way, and you're acceptable. Eat this food, like this music, play this sport, and you're a part of the in crowd. Deviate, and you're sitting alone at the lunch table.

As much as we like to think we mature out of this, most office cultures exhibit the same mentality. We punish, subtly or overtly, those who unsettle business as usual. There's a reason *The Office* ran for nine seasons, and why we place outliers like Apple on a pedestal.

The power of biology—our brain's synaptic pathway—coupled with the power of the status quo—our cultural pathway—is a formidable force. Most humans who try to push against that force will fail. It's just too damn hard. The world conspires against difference, and so does your brain. Everything is wired to keep you thinking right.

So how do these other humans manage it? How did Johannes Gutenberg, Pablo Picasso, Marie Curie, the Wright Brothers, Jane Goodall, Richard Dyson, Steve Jobs, Paul Farmer, and the ilk turn crazy ideas into inventions and movements that changed the world, while the rest of us struggle to escape the status quo?

They cultivated ways to challenge both their brains and the culture at large. They learned to think wrong, and so can you.

So can you.

Who Cares?

Okay. We've given you examples of remarkable people who are natural Wrong Thinkers. We've spoken directly to those of you who do not instinctively believe, in the words of Bessemer, that "whatever is, is right." But what about everyone else?

Well, there are five types of people in organizations who need to understand thinking wrong, and we've come to think of them as characters from the Wild West.

Outlaws

The innovators and disruptors who crave open space to explore new possibilities. Outlaws don't want to abide by the cultural norms of their organization. They are happy taking risks and being perceived of as outsiders operating at the edge.

Thinking wrong matters to Outlaws. It helps them ride beyond the status quo and defend themselves against ambushes and angry mobs.

Shepherds

The caretakers who protect Outlaws from those bent on stopping them. Shepherds provide Outlaws with the cover they need to explore, discover, and succeed. Shepherds also help get the products and services that Outlaws create to market without upending the rest of their organization.

Thinking wrong matters to Shepherds. It helps them lead and manage Outlaws—and keep Sheriffs and Posses from stringing up emerging solutions before they've had a chance to develop.

Scouts

The guides who help Shepherds and Outlaws navigate treacherous, uncharted paths, manage camps, and locate resources needed for these arduous journeys. Scouts lack ego, toil tirelessly, and go the extra mile to ensure fruitful explorations. They are often hired for their unique experience and knowledge of new territories.

Thinking wrong matters to Scouts. It helps them chart the most rewarding course and pack the right equipment and provisions for the adventure.

Sheriffs

The peace officers who enforce law and order within their organizations. Sheriffs make sure everything runs according to plan, that rules are followed, and that rabble-rousers are locked up or run out of town.

Thinking wrong matters to Sheriffs. It helps them demarcate the territories where Wrong Thinking is permitted and where Right Thinking is a must. Sheriffs are happy to enforce the right laws in the right places for the right reasons.

Posses

Most citizens in an organization want a peaceful life. They will follow the rules in order to fit in and reap the benefits of doing the right thing. They respond to the hue and cry and can be deputized to enforce the norms of their organizations, communities, or countries.

Thinking wrong matters to Posses. It clarifies the rightness of their efforts to keep things running well while helping them understand—and even support—the actions of Outlaws who are marking out the next territory for them to settle.

If you fill one or more of these roles in your organization, read on!

The
Elem
ents

of

Think
ing

Wro
ng

The Bold Path Is, By Definition, Abnormal

Taking the Bold Path

All of us find ourselves on the predictable path of how things have been, how things are, and how they will be. This status quo is forged by the synaptic connections in our brains and our cultural beliefs, biases, orthodoxies, and assumptions.

But, if you are like us, you are not content with the predictable path. You dare to look beyond the status quo. To imagine different outcomes than the one the predictable path leads to. So how do you forge a bold path? How do you take the Einsteinian, Steve Jobsian leap into the uncertain and unknown?

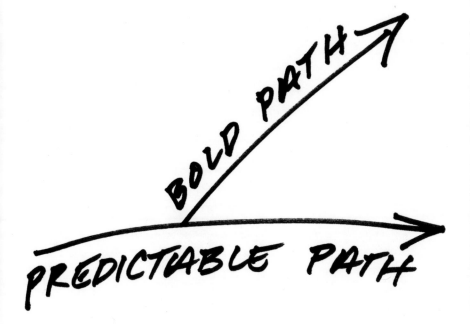

Every colleague we've ever worked with has had to fight to escape the powerful biological and cultural forces that have conspired to force them back into the status quo. Our Think Wrong Practices have grown from what we've learned from them. They, like better-known heroic geniuses, have found ways to blaze a bold path—and to resist snapping back to business as usual at critical moments in their journey to change and impact. To keep from conforming to the norm, you will need to be able to deflect from the status quo and protect yourself from the biological and cultural forces trying to pull you back in. You need to think wrong.

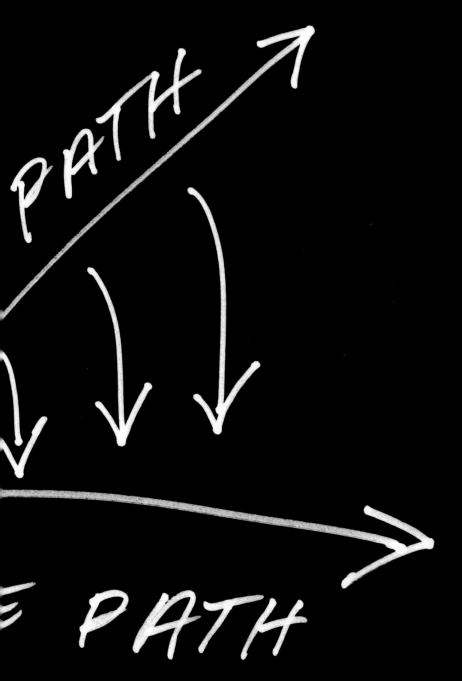

Your Brain and Culture Are Conspiring Against You

The human brain is amazing. It locks in what we experience and learn quickly, providing us with neural pathways that enable us to make quick, shortcut decisions and to take action without thinking or having to relearn simple tasks. This is a good thing. Imagine if we had to decide whether to brush our teeth each morning. And then had to Google: "How to brush my teeth."

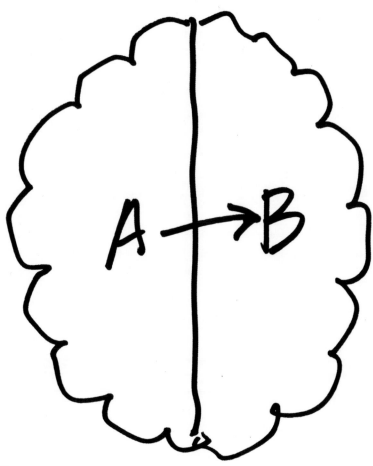

But our brains' ability to create these synaptic pathways has a downside, too. Those inner pathways govern everything we do—causing us to unknowingly repeat our problem-solving practices—resulting too often in predictable answers. We color inside the lines. We move from A to B.

The complications that arise from how we're biologically wired are compounded when a collection of brains is working in a social way. Group think becomes group belief. Group belief becomes dominant culture. What's acceptable, normal, and expected conspires against anything that lies beyond the status quo for organizations, communities, tribes, states, or nations.

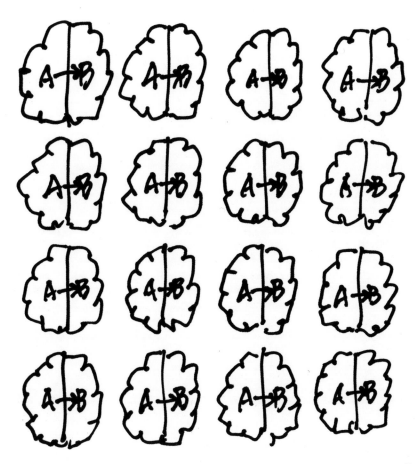

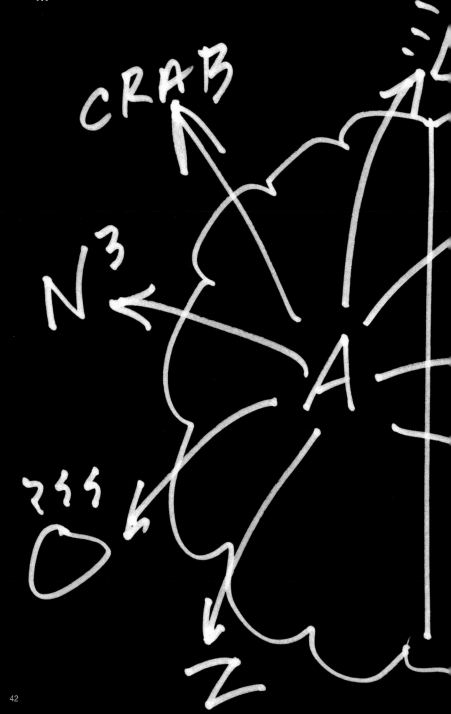

If you want to unleash your inner Picasso, if you want to go from A to Steaming Round Thing, you need to trick your brain. You need to let go of your beliefs, biases, orthodoxies, and assumptions. You need to start solving from a brand-new place. You need to think wrong.

Right Approach, Wrong Problem

Business schools and training programs perpetuate thinking right through the language, frameworks, tools, and techniques they teach. They focus on best practices, optimization, ROI, and metrics. They become the standard by which we are expected to measure pretty much everything, and it's become fashionable for people to assert that all types of institutions—schools, nonprofits, government agencies, and so on—should adopt Think Right Practices to become more efficient, more productive, and more effective.

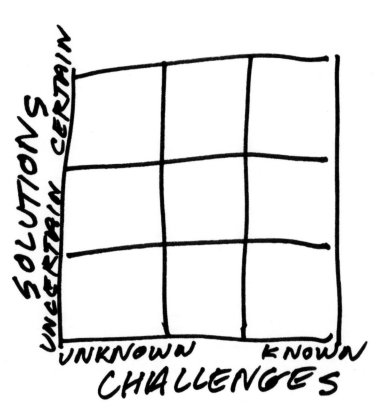

When you know the problem and are certain of the solution, the Think Right Practices are incredibly valuable. They provide managers (the Sheriffs) with a stabilizing structure and order. They lend rigor and discipline to how things get done. Costly distractions are avoided. Waste is reduced. Quality is improved. Productivity is increased. Solutions are scaled. The unintended cost? Crazy notions with the potential to drive massive impact are squashed before they even have a chance.

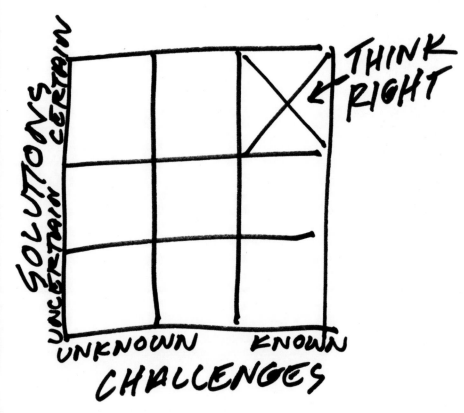

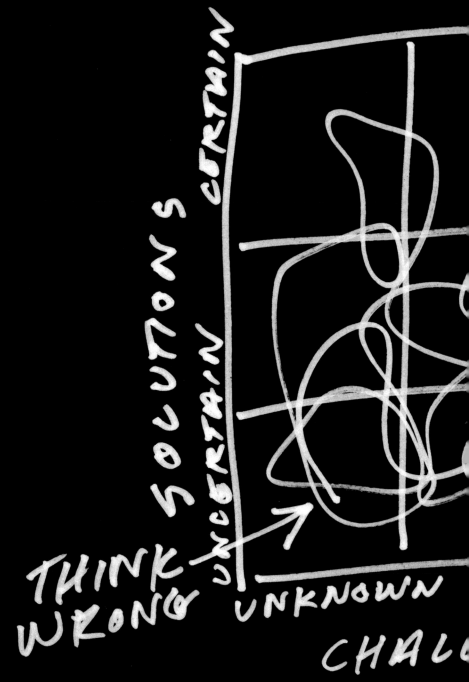

SOLUTIONS

CERTAIN

UNCERTAIN

THINK
WRONG

UNKNOWN

CHALL

THINK ← RIGHT

Learn to be honest about where your problem lies. How well do you understand it? And how certain are you of its solution? Sometimes, "Yes, I'll get right on that!" is the right answer. Other times, "Why?" is an even better one.

When it comes to exploring the unknown, adopt the mindset of a scientist or an artist. Start with a bold hypothesis or a compelling hunch. Then think wrong to navigate the uncertain and the unknown.

KNOWN

NGES

Think
Wrong
Practices

We've identified important moments
when the flame of possibility gets
extinguished. We've developed six
Think Wrong Practices that simulta-
neously advance compelling solutions
while defending them from attacks
by well-meaning Right Thinkers.
    We call these "practices" for a
reason. The more you do them, the
more resilient you become. Think
Wrong Practices foster a culture that
allows novel and compelling solutions
to be born, to thrive—or to be ruled

out because they do not work—in an affordable and swift way.

The beauty of these practices is that you can use them in combination or individually. As you become more adept with them, you'll find it helpful to apply one or two of them at critical moments in the discovery and development process. The Think Wrong Practices will help you to stay on the bold path and keep from slipping back into the status quo.

Critical Moment:
From Define to Dream

Be Bold.
Dare to make
a big difference.

Critical Moment:
From Research to Seek

Get Out.
Find fresh inspiration
for status quo–
busting solutions.

Critical Moment:
From Solve to Imagine

Let Go.
Stretch beyond
assumptions, biases,
and orthodoxies to
expand what's possible.

Critical Moment:
From Implement
to Explore

Make Stuff.
Gain insights
through making.

Critical Moment:
From Scale
to Experiment

Bet Small.
Discover what works
without risking it all.

Critical Moment:
From Defend to Share

Move Fast.
Be open so others can
help you improve your
solutions and achieve
impact sooner.

Think Wrong Drills

We've developed hundreds of drills to put the Think Wrong Practices in action. These drills give you counter-moves to the most common and tenacious biological and cultural challenges. They have been run successfully by everyone from the young designers who gave birth to PieLab in Belfast, Maine, to senior leaders at the White House, to teams of intrapreneurs disrupting the Global 1000 from the inside out.

You can use the Think Wrong Drills individually—or in bunches—when you want to depart from the predict-able solution path. We've been known to run as many as 15 in a day of Think Wrong Blitzing—intense, immersive, multi-day events designed to help organizations think wrong about a big challenge they are facing.

In the following chapters, we've selected three of our best drills for each practice. Consider the drills your recipe for thinking wrong. To get the most out of them, it helps to understand how they're organized.

1 Name of Drill
These vary from descriptive to playful—to evoke the nature of the drill and have a little fun.

2 When to Use
Describes the moment and the motivation you might have for running the drill.

3 Think Right
Predicts typical biological and cultural responses you might encounter.

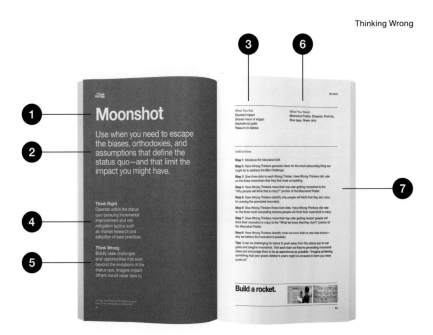

4 Think Wrong
Provides you with a counterpunch to Right Thinkers.

5 What You'll Get
Identifies the big outcome you can expect from the drill.

6 What You Need
We believe in having the right tools and materials for the job. This matters even more when you are asking people to step out of their comfort zone. Pre-printed posters, online resources and plentiful supplies provide reassurance, allow everyone to focus on the drill, and make it easier to capture and report the results.

7 Instructions
Step-by-step instructions on how to run the drill.

Many drills in our online Think Wrong Lab are accompanied by video clips that describe when to use the drill, how to introduce the drill, and tips and techniques for running the drill. They are also accompanied by galleries of photos illustrating the drills in action.

We provide you with free online resources at www.thinkwrongbook.com/resources to help you run the 18 drills featured in *Think Wrong*. These tools will help you put the book's ideas into action.

In the
Think Wrong
Universe:

Pie becomes an economic development tool. **A refreshing tonic fights human trafficking. An invasive crop of bamboo becomes an instrument for creating jobs and reducing traffic congestion and pollution. Playful drawings of bubbles spark a powerful ad campaign against Big Soda, obesity, and environmental degradation. A rock-and-roll-loving doctor helps turn a regulatory requirement into a tool to help cure cancer.** A global news giant learns to act like a start-up and builds an app to help tenants find their ideal commercial spaces.

You'll learn more
about these solutions
in the coming chapters,
but first we'd like to give
you a glimpse inside how
Think Wrong started for us.

Think Wrong

The Birth of Think Wrong

We created Future out of our own dissatisfaction with the status quo. Each one of us had been on the "right path." We were ascending our respective professions—John was an award-winning graphic designer, Greg was working for a top-tier global financial services firm, and Mike was told he could quickly become a young VP in his tech company (if only, he was told by a career coach, he would stop wearing a green watch and buy more Brooks Brothers pleated khakis).

We'd had it with conventional life. We felt stuck in a system that truncates connection and thoughtful work in deference to business as usual. As John once explained to *Metropolis* magazine: "I reached a certain point in my career. I could see the top, and it wasn't a peak worth climbing. I made a conscious shift in where I was trying to go, and it wasn't just about a successful career in graphic design, but something that, for me, was more meaningful."

In the 1990s, John and Greg first collaborated on a new vision for a creative services firm. They built a business that fostered a greater impact on the creative and professional lives of the people they partnered with—and the leaders they served—through intense collaboration.

In 2003, John took that desire a step further when he launched a side project called Project M. This immersive program shows young designers, writers, photographers, and filmmakers how to use their creativity to have significant

---

We felt stuck.

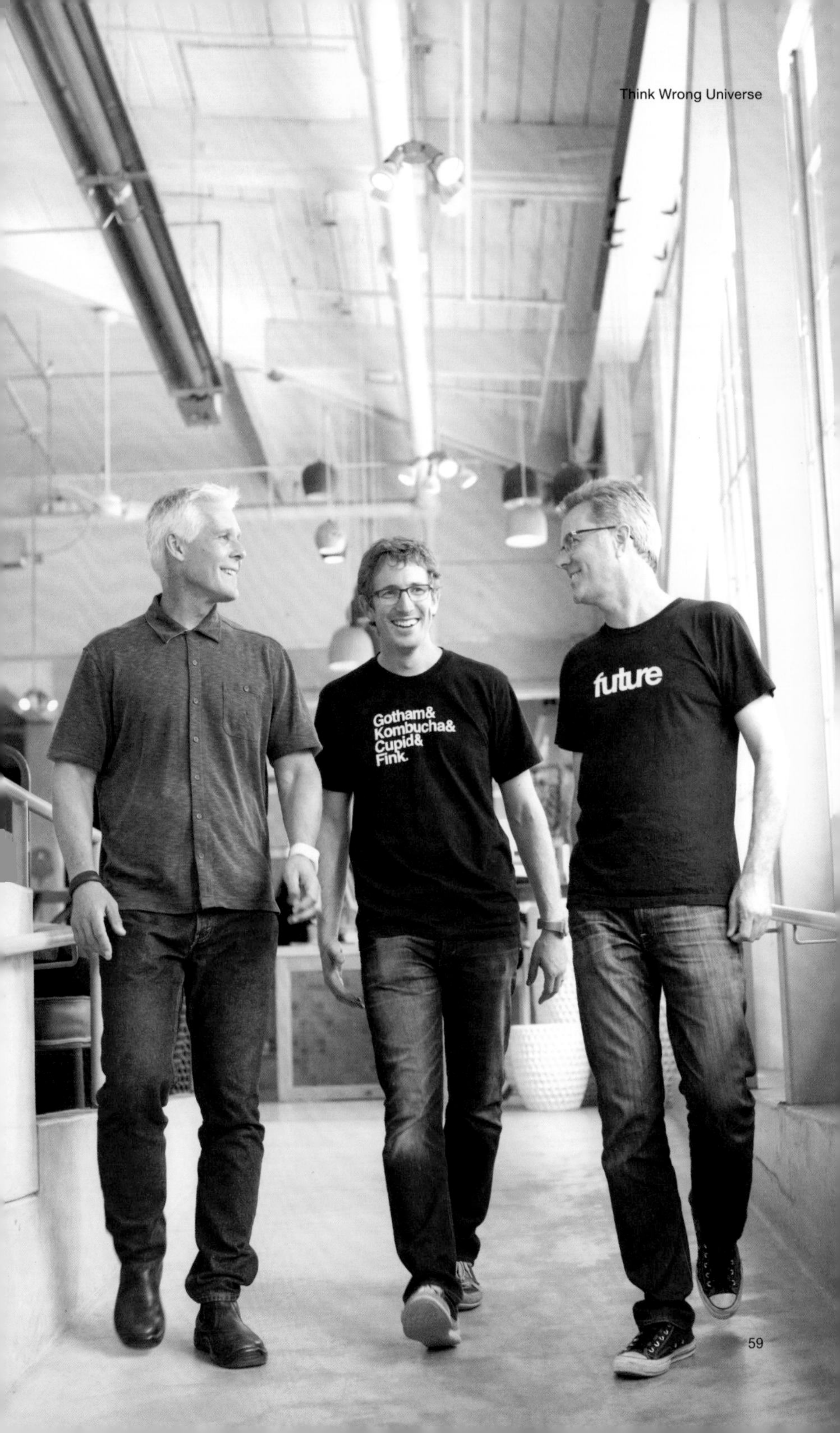
Gotham&
Kombucha&
Cupid&
Fink.
future

impact on communities around the globe. Project M has since sparked ingenious products, services, and start-ups from rural Alabama to Costa Rica and Iceland.

What we were learning from the forward-thinking ideas coming out of Project M soon infected the work of our firm. That's when we created Future, to encapsulate the best of both worlds. We wondered: What might happen if we could think wrong in business, government, foundations, and non-profits? How might we help the creative, passionate, committed, and often-frustrated leaders we were meeting transcend the biological and cultural resistance they were encountering so they might have a fighting chance at making the world a better place? How might we empower individuals and organizations through thinking wrong?

Over the years we have partnered with some of the most radical, outrageous, and experimental people in the world, and we've witnessed firsthand the power of thinking wrong. This book tells their stories. We've seen crazy ideas yield incredible results, and we have endeavored to study and understand the secrets and actions of those who successfully operate outside the predictable expectations of business and of culture. We began to see a connection in how these people behave and make decisions, in how they communicate their work, and in whom they deflect from the status quo.

1   2

1 Project M in Reykjavik, Iceland, gave the citizens of Iceland a way to express their discontent during their economic crisis in 2009. 2 Wrong Thinker Peter Coyote blitzing at the inception of Pando Populus, a forum to consider ecological alternatives to contemporary life.

Our gut told us something was going on here. Outlaws were able to overcome obstacles both in themselves and in the culture at large to achieve exceptional results. And they were most successful when the Shepherds, Scouts, Sheriffs, and Posses in their organizations were in on the game.

We have helped companies, universities, foundations, and nonprofits—from Microsoft and J.P. Morgan to the Robert Woods Johnson Foundation, the University of Notre Dame, the City of New York, and the White House—think wrong time and again. When people apply the practices, magic happens. They defy the pull of the status quo. They imagine new possibilities and implement bold solutions. They foster change and create results that make them proud and make a difference for others.

3   **4**

3 Thinking wrong about the future of shared work spaces with Global 1000 company Regus and Silicon Valley incubator and accelerator, mach49.
4 Thinking wrong about community banking with San Antonio Credit Union in San Antonio, Texas.

PieLab:
Thinking
Wrong
in Action

PIE LAB

1317

Closed

PIELAB, A STORY.

Closed

P

OPTIMIS

This is a story about thinking wrong.

This is also a story about pie.

Our story begins in March 2009 when a group of 14 young designers gathers in Belfast, Maine, for a Project M Blitz. The Blitz gets them out of their comfort zone and into a highly charged, multiday use of the Think Wrong Practices. These practices are crucial for you and your work, but we will get to them in a minute.

So here are these designers, freezing in Maine's version of "spring," and they have the task of generating a shared project that could do some good in the world. They need to do it quickly because this is a Blitz, after all, and as the word suggests, lightning fast is the name of the game. They have only a few days, but they can't figure out how to proceed. They're stuck, and being stuck, they do what all good souls do. They go to the bar.

Earlier that day, the group had performed one of the many Think Wrong Drills that we're going to share with you in this book. They answered the question: What is your secret talent? One graphic designer responded that she was really into pie. "Obsessed" was the word she used. She loves pie so much, in fact, that she orders a slice right then and there at the bar. Which is weird, right? Pie at a bar? But that's the level of commitment this young woman has to fruit encrusted in pastry dough. Plus, this is Maine. They serve pie at bars.

Which gets the group thinking: Really, who doesn't like pie?

This next part is going to sound cliché, but it's true: Someone finds a bar napkin, and the group starts sketching

They serve pie at bars.

ideas. They develop a simple hypothesis. Pie makes people happy. Being happy makes a person comfortable. Pie and coffee in the right setting could get people talking. Get people talking, and you learn things. Learn things, and you can help foster activities that effect positive change in a community.

It just so happens that March 14 is coming up—3.14, or π—and so they hatch a plan to host a free pie event in Belfast on international Pi Day. They invite the town for a slice and a cup of coffee.

Now John is the first to admit he thinks the idea is bonkers. How is free pie possibly going to manifest into a successful project for the greater good? But the designers are really engaged. This isn't a half-assed effort. So John keeps quiet; he lets go of his own think-right reaction; and he lets them do their thing. When March 14 rolls around, the event is a hit. People show up. So do newspaper reporters and television crews. John picks his chin up off the ground so that he, too, can eat some pie.

They debate where pie might have the most impact, and they decide to open a pop-up version in Greensboro, Alabama. Project M and John have a long relationship with HERO, a nonprofit run by Pam Dorr. HERO is a catalyst for community development in Greensboro with the goal of ending rural poverty. Pam says, "Yes, by all means, come open PieLab in Greensboro. In fact, I'll give you a place to do it." (Wrong Thinkers love people who say "yes." Pam always says "yes." Wrong Thinkers love Pam.)

1   **2**

1 Belfast townspeople show up for free pie on Pi Day, March 14, 2014. **2** Now every day is pie day in Greensboro, Alabama.

This is
the genesis
of PieLab.

The premise
is quite simple:

PieLab =
a neutral place +
a slice of pie.

A neutral place +
a slice of pie =
conversation.

Conversation =
ideas + design.

Ideas + design =
positive change.

That May, five of the designers drive south to set up shop in a small building, which is owned by HERO and located near the town's Main Street. It looked a bit like a one-room schoolhouse.

It's important to understand what these designers are heading into. Greensboro is the county seat of Hale County, one of the poorest places in the United States. The median household income is about $25,000. It was incorporated in 1823 and named for the then-famous Revolutionary War hero Nathanael Greene, who was known for saying, "We fight, get beaten, rise, and fight again."

The quote could be the mantra for Greensboro. That same ebb and flow of undulating fortunes has defined this rural Southern town. It has thrived; it has suffered; it has prospered from industry, lost it, and been hobbled by poverty. And it has fought, not just for its very survival, but also within its ranks. It is a town riven by race, class, and economics and marked by polarizing contrasts. It is home to affluent, majestic antebellum-era houses, but it is also where, in 1936, Walker Evans and James Agee took photos and wrote about dire poverty for the book *Let Us Now Praise Famous Men*. It is a place of long-held prejudices and civil rights activism, where, in March 1968, Martin Luther King, Jr., gave a rousing speech at a local church and then sought refuge from the Ku Klux Klan in a neighboring house. Greensboro is steeped in the past, but it is also home to the forward-thinking experimental architecture coming out of the Rural Studio cofounded by Samuel Mockbee.

1   **2**

1 Pam Dorr walked away from a successful career in fashion to work on ending rural poverty.
2 Pam's organization, HERO, provided the building for PieLab's first home.

In 2009, HERO was one of the few active businesses on Greensboro's Main Street. Vacant storefronts gave the place a ghost-town feel. Some buildings no longer had innards; they were just front-facing walls propped up by pilings. It was a Potemkin Village, with a facade of commerce but no real business.

The five designers arrive with very little money or readily obvious resources, but they are resourceful. They out the interior of this modest building on the cheap, buying plates and silverware from thrift stores, sourcing fruit and pecans from local farms, and building one long, family-style table from reclaimed wood. They make it a rule that pie is never for take-out. You have to eat in. As PieLab co-founder Brian Jones says, "PieLab provides a neutral environment in a segregated town where people from every race and class are welcome to sit together and talk about whatever is on their mind."

And that's just what happens. They put out a sandwich board advertising PieLab, and immediately, people show up. It's such a success the designers take the next step and, with the help of HERO, open a permanent shop on Main Street funded through a Kickstarter campaign. PieLab becomes the first new business to open on Main Street in years. They serve pie. They host events. Community groups meet there. Classes form. They support local pecan suppliers. It's more than pie; it's community building.

In the coming years, PieLab is nominated for a James Beard Award. It is lauded in publications from *The New York*

1   2

1 Today PieLab hosts open mike nights, art openings, and other local events. **2** PieLab now attracts both tourists and locals to a revitalized Main Street in rural Alabama.

Times to *Southern Living* to *Fast Company*. Most exciting, though, is the ripple effect it has on Greensboro. Today Main Street is witnessing a rebirth. New businesses are opening. A historic hotel, long vacant, is under renovation. Tour buses now transport people to Greensboro just for the chance to eat a piece of pie there.

How did this happen?

How did a cocktail-napkin sketch, very little money, and pie served in a pop-up shop turn into a permanent business on Main Street? How did PieLab became an economic catalyst for a struggling town and a cultural phenomenon capable of ameliorating long-held biases amid people who normally wouldn't associate with one another?

It's simple. PieLab is thinking wrong in action. The idea is bold, yet it evolved through a succession of small bets that minimized risk and allowed the founders to learn as they went, from the very people they hoped to engage. It involved getting out of their comfort zone, letting go of their biases, and making something with existing resources. PieLab also happened quickly. They moved fast, learned from their successes and failures, and kept evolving.

PieLab may have started in a seemingly random way— as a hidden talent that inspired a concept sketched on a napkin over pie and beers at a bar—but the truth is the idea was born out of a well-honed series of six practices and drills we have developed and tested over the years. And this is what we're here to teach you.

PieLab is thinking wrong in action.

1

Be Bold

"Proceed and be bold."

This was the mantra of the late, great architect Samuel
Mockbee, co-founder of the Rural Studio in Hale County,
Alabama. John first heard Mockbee speak of his bold vision
for architecture during a lecture at the California College of
the Arts in San Francisco back in 2000. Mockbee walked
on stage looking like anything but an architect. No wire rim
glasses. No slick slacks. Sambo, as his friends called him,
was a bear of a guy, bearded and casual and dressed in a
rumpled sport coat. A thick, Southern accent warmed the
deep timbre of his voice.

Mockbee opened his talk by showing a short, homemade movie. Up on the screen came the image of a preacher
from Hale County who had taught his pigs to pray before
eating. The pigs were poised at the trough, porcine heads
bowed, until the preacher shouted "Amen!" and they snuffled
to feed. That film, Mockbee said, offered an inside look at
the community where he and his architecture students
worked. It was so unexpected, so strangely powerful.
John was hooked.

Mockbee went on to explain how the Rural Studio took
architecture students from Auburn University out of the classroom and into rural Hale County. They lived and worked and
broke bread with some of the poorest people in the country.
Together they designed and built incredible structures,
providing what Mockbee called "an architecture of decency."

It is also an architecture based in thinking wrong.
Mockbee eschewed the typical pedagogy—which cloisters
students on campus and keeps them working on theoretical

Proceed and be bold.

concepts—and upended the traditional patronage model of the client–architect relationship. He reimagined the way in which buildings could get made with limited time and money. His students fabricated houses out of unused FLOR carpet tiles and rammed earth, chapels out of old car windshields, smokehouses out of recycled glass bottles. In the process, Mockbee connected these kids to people they would never normally interact with, and he introduced them to the depth of their humanity. He showed these budding architects their capacity to change lives and to practice architecture in unorthodox ways.

Nobody told Sam Mockbee he had to go out and create a legendary design-build program to address rural poverty. He had been asked, along with Auburn professor D.K. Ruth, to create a study abroad program. Mockbee's genius was in questioning the very fundamentals of how that might happen. Instead of sending students to far-flung cultures, Mockbee believed that "abroad" could be in the university's backyard. He understood that the power to change lives, along with the pedagogy of architecture, lay in a landscape a mere three hours away.

The Be Bold Practice is designed to help you tap into that same powerful goal-setting principle.

Why Be Bold?
Mockbee was handed a task, but rather than take a predictable route, he asked: *Why must a study abroad program be abroad?*

1   2

1 A community gathering space in Mason's Bend, Alabama made from recycled car windows.
2 Surplus FLOR carpet tiles are stacked to make the walls of a house, also in Mason's Bend.

Mockbee allowed himself to question the assignment as presented. And then he allowed himself to dream big about what that program might accomplish. Thinking right would have meant accepting the challenge as given. Thinking wrong reframed the opportunity for greater impact.

The practice of Be Bold supports the pivotal "Dream" moment. This is a crucial time, yet too often we brush right through it in our rush to be finished. We're trapped in top-down hierarchies and command-and-control cultures that tell us not to ask too many questions. Don't rock the boat. Don't ask why. Just get on with it already.

The path to a genius solution, though, starts with discovering your true challenge. Be Bold Drills get you questioning the way things are and prime you for how things might ideally be. Taking a moment to examine and set intention—and to aspire to a greater result—stretches the realm of possibilities and immediately changes the mindset around your work. Be Bold helps you frame the challenge or opportunity you want to address and define the difference you hope to make. The drills in this chapter will help you and your team to aim higher and embolden everyone to consider the purpose and meaning of your work.

Here's what you're up against. Culturally, bold ideas scare people. They feel foreign, unsafe, nebulous. (Think what a lawyer might have advised when Mockbee suggested setting college kids loose with power tools in a rural back-water.) They can also feel like a distraction from getting things done and go against a culture in which questions are not valued.

Bold ideas scare people.

Bold questions and challenges are daunting because our brains are forever weighing what one neurologist dubs the "carrot of desire against the whip of fear." We worry that our vision won't find support in our organization. And we're not wrong here. We frequently have conversations with executives and leaders in which we challenge them to be honest about whether their stated visions, missions, and strategic imperatives align with how people are rewarded and recognized inside their organization. Too often there's a disconnect. And people won't dare to make a difference if the culture doesn't encourage doing so.

Be Bold Drills upset these dynamics by creating playful, respectful, and productive environments within which you and your team can aspire to more. Be Bold Drills move you away from small solutions and incremental improvement so you may take big leaps.

Getting Into the Be Bold Mindset
There is rarely a "Dream" moment in the world of right thinking. Thinking right about a challenge or an opportunity means doing what you are told, focusing on the bottom line at the expense of game-changing solutions, and going along to get along.

The following drills will help you Be Bold.

1   2

1 College of Creative Studies students launch the Detroit Space Program to reclaim abandoned spaces. **2** Faceball makes learning literacy sight words fun for kids and their families in Long Island City, New York.

Be Courageous.
Dare to imagine the
biggest difference
you might make.

Be Idealistic.
Consider your legacy.
What's worthy of
your life's work?

Be Challenging.
Refuse to accept
the mandate of
the status quo.

Deflection Point

Use when you want to explore the difference you might make.

Think Right
Optimize the status quo.

Think Wrong
Depart from the status quo to change things from how they are to how they should be.

For free Think Wrong Drill Resources go to:
www.thinkwrongbook.com/resources

What You Get

Insights into the way things are and how they might be

Identification of useful trends and global forces that might be leveraged

People and partners are emotionally and functionally engaged

What You Need

Large empty area on wall or floor, Sharpies, Post-its, Blue tape

Instructions

Step 1 Introduce the Deflection Point Drill.

Step 2 Ask Wrong Thinkers to make a horizontal line on the wall with blue painter's tape. Have them write "The Predictable Path" on the line with a Sharpie. Explain that this line represents the status quo.

Step 3 Using Post-its, ask Wrong Thinkers to describe "The Predictable Path" (e.g., vulnerable food supply, disconnect between food and seed, general apathy, etc.).

Step 4 Using the blue tape, have teams create a new line coming off "The Predictable Path" at a 45° angle, and label it "The Bold Path."

Step 5 Using Post-its, ask Wrong Thinkers to describe "The Bold Path" (e.g., sustainable food supply, a clear connection between food and seed, real interest among the public, etc.).

Step 6 Using Post-its, have Wrong Thinkers identify trends that might be used to drive the shift from "The Predictable Path" to "The Bold Path" (e.g., technological trends, social trends, cultural trends, economic trends, etc.). Have Wrong Thinkers place these Post-its in the space between "The Bold Path" and "The Predictable Path."

Step 7 Place a long, horizontal strip of blue tape on the wall or floor. Have Wrong Thinkers sort "The Bold Path" Post-its into categories (e.g., Customers, Operations, Policies, Partnerships, etc.) above the line of tape. Make sure they label the categories. Label the area above the line "To."

Step 8 Have Wrong Thinkers sort "The Predictable Path" Post-its in the same categories below the line of blue tape. Label the area below the line "From."

Set brazen goals.

Moonshot

Use when you need to escape the biases, orthodoxies, and assumptions that define the status quo—and that limit the impact you might have.

Think Right
Operate within the status quo pursuing incremental improvement and risk mitigation tactics such as market research and adoption of best practices.

Think Wrong
Boldly seek challenges and opportunities that exist beyond the limitations of the status quo. Imagine impact others would never dare to.

For free Think Wrong Drill Resources go to:
www.thinkwrongbook.com/resources

What You Get
Elevated impact
Shared vision of impact
Aspirational goals
Reasons to believe

What You Need
Moonshot Poster, Sharpies, Post-its,
Blue tape, Green dots

Instructions

Step 1 Introduce the Moonshot Drill.

Step 2 Have Wrong Thinkers generate ideas for the most astounding thing they might do to address the Blitz Challenge.

Step 3 Give three dots to each Wrong Thinker. Have Wrong Thinkers dot vote on the three moonshots that they find most compelling.

Step 4 Have Wrong Thinkers move their top vote-getting moonshot to the "Why people will think that is crazy" portion of the Moonshot Poster.

Step 5 Have Wrong Thinkers identify why people will think that they are crazy for pursing the promoted moonshot.

Step 6 Give Wrong Thinkers three more dots. Have Wrong Thinkers dot vote on the three most compelling reasons people will think their moonshot is crazy.

Step 7 Have Wrong Thinkers move their top vote-getting reason people will think their moonshot is crazy to the "What we know that they don't" portion of the Moonshot Poster.

Step 8 Have Wrong Thinkers identify what we know that no one else knows— why we believe the moonshot is possible.

Tips It can be challenging for teams to push away from the status quo to set goals and imagine moonshots. Visit each team as they're generating moonshot ideas and encourage them to be as aspirational as possible: "Imagine achieving something that your grandchildren's peers might be amazed to learn you were a part of."

Build a rocket.

Challenge the Challenge

Use when you want to encourage, build, and grow a culture that questions the way things are.

Think Right
Accept the challenge as given.

Think Wrong
Push back and challenge.

What You Get
Multiple entry points for addressing a challenge or an opportunity that matters

People you want to serve are identified

What You Need
Challenge the Challenge Poster, Sharpies, Post-its, Blue tape

Instructions

Step 1 Introduce the Challenge the Challenge Drill.

Step 2 Have Wrong Thinkers reframe the challenge statement to reflect the greatest impact the team might hope to have.

Step 3 Ask each team to share their new challenge statement with the group.

Embrace your inner teen.

The Story of REBBL

Be Bold in Action

Creating a healthy beverage isn't revolutionary. Using it to fight human trafficking?

That's thinking wrong.

In 2000, entrepreneur David Batstone was shocked to learn that his favorite restaurant in the San Francisco Bay Area had served as a hub for human trafficking. David decided to be courageous and travel the world for five years to understand the forces behind trafficking. He then wrote a book about what he learned, *Not For Sale: The Return of the Global Slave Trade—and How We Can Fight It*, and founded Not For Sale, a nonprofit aimed at freeing the more than 30 million people worldwide forced to work for little or no pay.

One place Not For Sale focused its efforts is Madre de Dios, a 200-square-kilometer area of rainforest in the Peruvian Amazon. This is one of the most ecologically vibrant places in the world, and yet the people who live there are incredibly poor because they are removed from economic marketplaces. Both the people and the environment are exploited by human traffickers preying on the villagers' need for a livelihood. "We knew there had to be a solution to that problem. The only question was, 'What would that solution be?'" David says.

In 2011, we worked with David and his team to frame a question around that bold challenge. We asked: How might we use social enterprise to help disrupt the exploitation of villagers and their environment in this region of the Peruvian Amazon?

Traditional answers to this question might include stricter governmental regulation and oversight, more think tanks on the subject, international conferences aimed at incremental changes over enforcement. We took a different approach.

We took a different approach.

During a two-day Think Wrong Blitz held in Montara, California, we gathered a group of diverse individuals—doctors, scientists, lawyers, agronomists, healthcare entrepreneurs, even the famed baseball player Jeremy Affeldt, relief pitcher for the San Francisco Giants. Not For Sale had launched its nonprofit from a bold proposition—ending human trafficking. The trick was to encourage bold thinking among the assembled leaders and bring the creative ingenuity and resources of their unique talents to bear on this task. So how do you engage a diverse group quickly around such a lofty goal? Jeremy, for example, couldn't understand initially why he had been invited. "I didn't go to college. I signed out of high school," he said. "I don't have a business degree. I was out of place, and I didn't feel like I had anything to offer."

First, we used Be Bold Drills to let the myriad professionals dream about the difference they might make in the lives of people living in the Peruvian Amazon. Soon they could imagine why they might marshal their resources to end human trafficking in the seven villages in Madre de Dios.

Next, we broke the group into small teams and asked each to think of the situation in Madre de Dios as an entrepreneurial opportunity rather than a trafficking problem. We asked them to compete with one another and come up with a venture that might give the villagers economic independence. We ran Simply Epic, a Be Bold Drill that asks: What's the simplest thing you can imagine that will have the most profound impact?

1   2

1 Mark Wexler and David Batstone founded Not For Sale to end modern-day slavery for more than 30 million people. 2 Montara Circle, a Think Wrong Blitz, convened diverse leaders to disrupt the exploitation of people and planet.

One participant, an oncologist, noted the health benefits of Cat's Claw, which is prevalent in the Peruvian Amazon. Something clicked for Jeremy. "I was drinking tea, and I said, 'Hey, can we make this a tea?'" The Be Bold Practice allowed Jeremy to reframe the challenge in his own mind, which opened all kinds of possibilities for him.

More questions soon followed: Why are villagers and their environment being exploited? Why do others have greater rights to the minerals and plants in their homeland and forests? Why are they dependent on a single boatman to bring their goods to market?

Jeremy's group spent the next hour envisioning a beverage company that lets the villagers harvest healthful ingredients from the Amazon for a drink, and that idea ultimately became REBBL Tonic (standing for "Roots, Extracts, Berries, Bark, and Leaves"). By 2014, REBBL reached a new sales high of $205,000 in just one month. People from seven villages in the Madre de Dios region now have greater economic security through contracts with fair trade and organic exporters to provide Cat's Claw and other ingredients. In return, REBBL gives a share of its profits to other Not For Sale efforts. Today millions of consumers are able to participate in eradicating human trafficking by buying a drink.

Hey, can we make this a tea?

This bold idea never could have happened without first overcoming the reaction most people have about fighting human trafficking: It's too big, too dark, too complex an issue. There's also the cultural assumption that victims of trafficking somehow allow themselves to be exploited, and that government and law enforcement agencies should be fixing the problem. When we invited people to dream about what might be possible, and then connected them in a human way to the impact they might have on the lives of the villagers of Madre de Dios, we were able to unlock a groundswell of ingenious ideas.

The power of thinking wrong, and of the Think Wrong Practices, is that the outcome isn't always a recognizably outrageous result. Come across a bottle of REBBL chilling in a cold case at your local Whole Foods, and you wouldn't think to yourself, "Well that's insane!" Nope—you'd see another healthy beverage option. A beverage product, however, is a surprising way to fight human trafficking. The only way Not For Sale got to this answer was by being bold enough to think wrong about how we might fight slavery in the modern age.

1   **2**

1 Jeremy Affeldt went from pitching the World Series to launching a slavery-fighting social enterprise. 2 Today REBBL is sold across the U.S., generating funds to end human trafficking in the Peruvian Amazon.

Think
Wrong

2

Get Out

Several years ago we were invited to JP Morgan Chase in New York for a meeting. We'd already worked with the Treasury Group at JP Morgan to teach them how to think wrong about the global launch of an important new product, and it had turned out well. As a result, we were recommended to their colleagues at the financial giant.

We arrived at the company's headquarters in Midtown Manhattan, and the first thing that greeted us outside was a phalanx of armed guards clutching leashed security dogs. Inside were more armed guards and a security desk, where we turned over IDs, answered questions, and received identification badges. We wove through turnstiles, careful to scan our badges, and took an escalator up to a mezzanine where we found ourselves deposited in a massive, multistoried lobby. Professionals in suits read newspapers and drank coffee as they waited to be called to the upper floors of the skyscraper and conduct business. Above their heads, mounted high on the wall, were two enormous Jumbotrons—the kind you'd find in a stadium—and on the 40-foot screens were these words: "Fostering a Culture of Innovation."

Next we took an elevator to a conference room and were met by six people circling a large table. A seventh person beamed in live from London. We had barely sat down when one of our hosts said, "You have 20 minutes to convince us why we should hire you." Welcome to the innovation team for JP Morgan's Treasury Group.

Fostering a Culture of Innovation.

Get Out

Instead of pitching our firm, Greg decided to tell a story. He talked about thinking wrong and, in particular, our Get Out Practice. This practice began with Project M. John had noticed that Project M was such a success, in part, because it placed participants in unfamiliar locations. Being in a new setting enhanced both the quality of their output and their overall experience. It makes sense, right? When we are outside our normal routine, we become more alert, more engaged. Think about your commute to work. How many times have you arrived at the office having forgotten the act of getting there? Compare that with navigating a new city. You're taking everything in, alert to your surroundings, because everything is new. This is why we never conduct a Think Wrong Blitz onsite at a client's office, and why you never should, either. Nor do we host events in hotels or conference rooms. Those spaces are equally familiar and deadening. People tune out, which means they are less receptive to inspiration.

Greg finished explaining this practice, then he turned to our hosts and asked, "Do you know what's written on the Jumbotrons in your lobby?"

They looked at one another. Shook heads.

He asked, "Are you sure? No idea?"

Blank looks all around. They were stumped.

"It reads: 'Fostering a Culture of Innovation,'" Greg said.

The innovation team laughed. They had no idea because they had completely tuned out their surroundings.

Everything is new.

Why Get Out?

It's so easy to get stuck in routine. Familiar environments cause the brain to tune out, to be less alert and less receptive to new input. Our instinct for survival sometimes keeps us from exploring the unknown and biases us to the familiar.

This is why vacation is such a wondrous thing. Removed from our quotidian existence, we reconnect to our basic senses. The world opens up, and we notice things again. The rhythmic pound of surf on sand, the street art brightening a cobbled alley, the smells of exotic food in a foreign market. We return home renewed and ready to tackle the world. And yet it takes just a few days to get sucked right back into the routine and the tunnel vision.

It's a common complaint that we silo disciplines and stunt collaboration with rigid job descriptions. And yet, we silo our own lives as well, keeping our variant selves packed into confined and tidy categories. There's the person we are at work, at home, on vacation. What if we carried that mindful, alert, explorative "vacation" self into our everyday lives?

Get Out Drills support the "Seek" moment, when you decide where your inspiration and guidance will come from.

Who and what will inform your decision-making? Culturally, you're going to have to battle Right Thinkers who want you to hunker down and talk to the experts, read reports, seek best practices that worked in the past, gather data, and then, perhaps, bring in a focus group to weigh in.

1   2

1 An opium farmer in Yangon, Myanmar, provides new insight into the criminalization of production and the punishment of addicts. 2 A resilient family in New Orleans, Louisiana, inspires financial solutions to help people get back in their homes.

Personally, you want to prime your mind to support serendipity. Our brains are inquisitive, curious, often at work on a task even unconsciously. We like to think that epiphanies—like the apple clocking Newton on the head—are the things that lead to the big breakthroughs, but the truth is that putting yourself in the path of something new helps to trigger the brain's powers of connectivity.

The Get Out Practice reopens the aperture in your mind. It primes you to take in new information and make surprising and serendipitous connections along the way. Get Out assumes no given starting point. Instead you approach this moment ready to discover new sources for inspiration and influence. You leave the confines of your office, studio, or home and explore the unknown. In doing so, you create opportunities for true discovery.

Get Out Drills also encourage connection with real people in the real world. We partner with clients all over the world, and we have a get out ethos to stay where we work. We sleep on pull-out sofas. We pad down the halls of our hosts' homes in our PJs and share a breakfast table with their kids. We've rented houses through Airbnb in the neighborhoods impacted by the work we're charged with doing. We do this because we believe in being in the community we hope to

1   2

We sleep on pull-out sofas.

solve problems with. This helps to connect problems and potential solutions in a way that you can't achieve from the isolation of your office. Human-to-human contact is invaluable; otherwise, your solution runs the risk of being academic, disconnected, and in the worst instances, brutal.

Getting Into the Get Out Mindset

When it's time to draw inspiration for solutions, to start to flesh them out and see what they might be, people rarely gather the team and leave the office to go somewhere. Usually it's about getting right down to business.

The following drills will help you Get Out.

3   4

1 Systemspotting at Institut Pasteur in Abidjan. **2** Enlisting artists, gamers, designers, and youth in Detroit to fight Big Tobacco. **3** Discovering who matters to the future of San Antonio Credit Union. **4** San Francisco garden center reframes what co-working space might look like.

Be Adventurous.
Seek inspiration in new people, new places, and new experiences—rather than revisiting all the usual suspects.

Be Attentive.
Pay close attention to what's going on—looking for, listening for, smelling, and feeling what's new— and collect the most compelling things as fresh inspiration.

Be Receptive.
Accept every offer without judgment and with an eye toward expanding what might be possible.

3x3x3

Use when you need to break through preconcep-tions, elitism, and status that restrict what might be considered.

Think Right
Defer to industry experts, data, and best practices.

Think Wrong
Seek inspiration from unex-pected people and places.

What You Get
An attentive, receptive,
collaborative mindset

Serendipitous connections
and insights

Team bonding and boldness

What You Need
3x3x3 Poster, Pens, Sharpies,
Notebooks, Post-its, Blue tape

Instructions

Step 1 Introduce the 3x3x3 Drill.

Step 2 Have Wrong Thinkers pair up.

Step 3 Have Wrong Thinkers explore the area surrounding the Blitz and ask them to go to three places, meet three people, and come back with three stories.

Step 4 Invite duos to share their stories with the group.

Step 5 As a group, discuss reflections, insights, and implications.

Tips We often find it is helpful to provide Wrong Thinkers with an opening question to ask people when they get out.

Be inspired.

Think
Wrong

That's Odd

Use when you need to start solving from an entirely new place.

Think Right
Start solving from what
is known and proven.

Think Wrong
Find a completely random
place to start solving from.

For free Think Wrong Drill Resources go to:
www.thinkwrongbook.com/resources

What You Get
An attentive, receptive,
and collaborative mindset

Random starting places

Greater opportunity for serendipitous
connections

Team bonding and increased boldness

What You Need
That's Odd Poster, Smartphone,
Pens, Sharpies, Post-its,
Notebooks, Brown paper bag

Instructions

Step 1 Introduce the That's Odd Drill.

Step 2 Have Wrong Thinkers pair up.

Step 3 Send Wrong Thinkers out to identify the three strangest things they can find in the surrounding environment.

Step 4 Ask Wrong Thinkers to email or text photographs of what they find to you.

Step 5 When they return, have Wrong Thinkers write the three strangest things on separate Post-its using only 1–2 words to describe each thing.

Step 6 Ask Wrong Thinkers to place those Post-its in a brown paper bag. (Use with the Random Word Drill in Chapter 3).

Step 7 Ask several teams to share the highlights from their That's Odd adventure.

Get weird.

Silent Walk

Use when you want thoughtful reflections on ideas, activities, conversations, emerging solutions, and progress.

Think Right
Push to next take or answer.

Think Wrong
Step away from the challenge, allowing time to process what is happening and what matters most.

What You Get
An attentive, receptive,
and collaborative mindset

Observations, insights,
serendipitous connections

Reflection, inspiration, and enriched
understanding of opportunity.

What You Need
Silent Walk Poster, Sharpies,
Post-its, Blue tape

Instructions

Step 1 Introduce the Silent Walk Drill.

Step 2 Have Wrong Thinkers pair up. Invite Wrong Thinkers to reflect on
the conversations and Think Wrong Drills.

Step 3 Have Wrong Thinkers walk in silence near the Blitz location.

Step 4 Have Wrong Thinkers share their reflections, capturing highlights
on the Silent Walk Poster.

Walk softly.

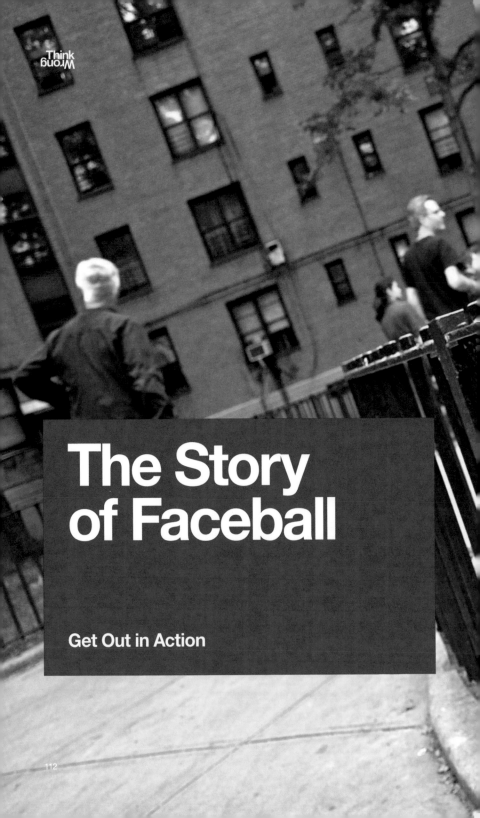

The Story of Faceball

Get Out in Action

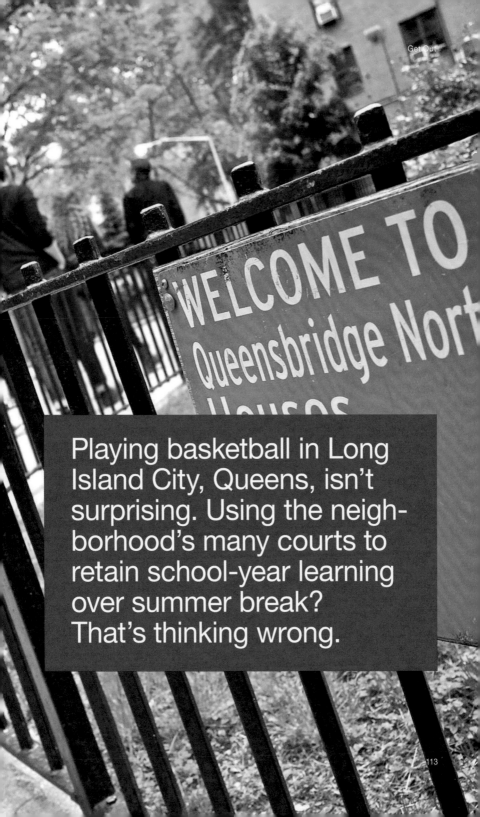

Playing basketball in Long Island City, Queens, isn't surprising. Using the neighborhood's many courts to retain school-year learning over summer break? That's thinking wrong.

It's a summer day in Long Island City, Queens, and competing teams meet on a basketball court. Two young players, secondary-school students from the Queensbridge neighborhood, stand at center court. Instead of a tip-off to start the game, a referee asks, "What's the capital of Delaware?"

The players sprint to their respective hoops, where teammates shout out the answer "Dover! It's Dover!"

The player with the ball scans round plates scattered across the court. Each plate is inscribed with a letter, and he must find the right ones to spell out the answer. He sees "D" sprints to it and shoots. He makes it, and his team cheers. They point to the "O," and he runs to that letter, shoots, and misses. His teacher shouts, "You've got this! Try again!" He shoots, and this time—nothing but net.

Welcome to Faceball, a new game that's teaching literacy to students in a neighborhood where summer learning isn't a given.

Queensbridge is home to the largest public-housing development in North America. Here the average family income is about $23,000 a year. Like all parents, those living in Queensbridge want the best for their children, but they aren't always in a position to help. English may be a second language; jobs can trump family time. Helping with homework may get tricky when the child's curriculum surpasses that of the parent's education. Then there's summer. School's out, so how do you keep a kid from losing ground in the months away from the classroom? How do you keep them learning?

Dover!
It's Dover!

In May 2014, we gathered in Queensbridge to work with the New York City Department of Education's Family and Community Engagement team and Lonni Tanner, chief at the Office of Public Imagination for the New York City Department of Probation (really, you should check out her work). Our three-day Think Wrong Blitz aimed to generate ingenious solutions to this question: *How might we get parents and children to engage in learning and literacy through a super-simple, really cool, low-cost summer program?*

We wanted to remove barriers for parents and allow them to participate in their child's learning. We wanted kids to easily absorb and retain the alphabet as well as Fry sight words, which are those common words necessary to build reading fluency and navigate the world. We also wanted to develop a way for the community as a whole to support this effort. Oh, and we wanted to do it fast: The goal was to have some kind of program running by July.

Our initial Get Out Drill helped gel the team—composed of educators, designers, parents, and neighbors—and bond them around the task at hand. One team member was New York–based illustrator and graphic designer John Custer. We asked John to participate in the Blitz as an Outsider. We often bring in orthogonal thinkers and creative makers to get our clients out of their normal routine.

"That first day, you get introduced to all these new people," John says, "and you work really hard, and your brain kind of hurts from all this quick thinking. That's when Future asks you to pause and get away and get to know

1   2

So many courts, so many kids.

your team. You were strangers a few hours ago, but then you take a break, get some fresh air, ask questions, and create a tighter-knit group."

Next we let Queensbridge residents and neighbors inform and inspire us. We walked the streets and met local leaders, librarians, businesspeople, and kids. We interviewed them and invited them back to work with our team. We discovered all of the available resources in the community that might be used to support literacy learning.

The idea of basketball emerged quickly. There are so many courts, and so many kids who want to play. What if we hacked the classic game of Horse—where you shoot from various spots on a court to spell that word—and turned it into a literacy game instead? Faceball (short for Family and Community Engagement, the New York City Department of Education group that had engaged us) was born.

Within days, the game was being tested in gyms, on basketball courts, in schools. The initial prototype involved spelling, but teachers quickly adapted it to include lessons in geography and math. Andre Stith, a teacher, says Faceball "just clicked" for everyone. "It's a no-brainer that this would teach the kids and be implemented all over," he says.

Rather than hunkering down in a fluorescent-lit conference room, Lonni got these educators out into their community and created something affordable and fast to support summertime literacy—a game that gets the whole community out and rallying their kids to succeed.

3　　　　**4**

1 Teachers hacked Faceball to teach more than reading. 2 Gathering wisdom from longtime Queensbridge residents. 3 Parents in Queensbridge want the best for their children. 4 Words are everywhere in Long Island City.

3

Let

Go

Syphilis Biscuit.

We'll get to that seemingly insane phrase in a second. First, we want to talk about decision-making.

The funny thing about human beings is that we frequently make decisions against our best interests. We'll stay at our current job even though a preferable one exists. We'll invest money in the wrong retirement plan simply because our co-workers picked that one. We'll choose an existing option over finding a potentially better alternative because the former is familiar. We do this because of our heuristic and status quo biases.

The three of us talk about the status quo in this book so much because the pull of the accepted norm is very real. Everyone from behavioral economists to psychologists to neurologists has studied the human relationship with the status quo, and empirical evidence shows we have a proclivity to place value on the way things are currently done. We believe something is more valid simply because it already exists.

We're also fighting against heuristics, which are our preset patterns of thinking—those synaptic circuit connections we develop. Our brain weighs certain information based on experience, and we act on these shortcuts. Our colleague and friend, the neurologist Marc Diamond, refers to these shortcuts as our brain's "narratives."

"It's fundamental in our nervous system to save time and be efficient by creating the neural equivalent of narratives, or patterns that we respond to," Marc says. "These shortcuts

Watch a little kid learning to walk.

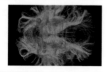

are important to our efficiency. If you watch a little kid learning to walk, for instance, it requires a lot of mental effort."

The danger with heuristics and status quo bias is that the same thinking yields the same results. Our narratives perpetuate existing conditions and cause us, consciously or unconsciously, to limit possibility. If you've successfully solved a problem in the past, it's not surprising that you'll jump to that same methodology in the future. If the boss is squeamish of risk, it's understandable when tepid ideas are presented at staff meetings. Meanwhile, the brilliant answers you require might exist outside conventional thinking. "These narrative shortcuts make us work much more efficiently, and mostly they're good," Marc says. "But when you're trying to do something different—something innovative— they impede you."

Heuristics and status quo bias are the death of wild and crazy ideas, and wild and crazy ideas are the ones that lead to high-impact solutions. For example, a guy like Elon Musk might wonder, "What if we could mitigate our reliance on fossil fuels and power our entire lives with batteries?" It takes a leap of creative imagination to meet this challenge— and requires that we let go of a whole bunch of assumptions and beliefs.

The Let Go Practice was developed to prevent our clients from snapping back to the same old thinking when presented with new challenges. The Let Go Drills spark unexpected output by forcing people to solve challenges differently. Here's an example. A few years ago, we were

Spark unexpected output.

hired by Thomas Sevcik of the Zurich-based strategy firm Artheisa to help a very smart team of marketing and PR professionals working for Deutsche Bank. We gathered in Manhattan for a Think Wrong Blitz focused on how the bank might change the way it relates to its customers. We began by asking the team members to list every single communications tactic they'd ever used. They wrote each on a Post-it and stuck it to the wall, and soon the room was fluttering with hundreds of colored pieces of paper. It was a big list. These people knew the means of branding and promoting a major financial institution, and they were clearly proud of this prowess; we could see that. Then we said, "Great. Those are verboten. Throw them away because you can no longer use them."

It looked like their heads might pop. And that's pretty much the point of Let Go. To blow up your brain's shortcut narratives and assumptions. When you let go, you move beyond the knowns, and you start generating more ideas than you think possible from a completely new place. The Let Go Drills challenge you to open your mind and turn off the biases built into that highly efficient brain of yours. It means silencing your inner devil's advocate. The goal is to keep playing, keep producing ideas, and stop worrying about finding the *right* answer. That comes later.

So when you run a Let Go Drill such as Random Word, where arbitrary words are mashed together, and you require participants to use only the resultant phrases as the springboard for a solution, you'll be amazed where something

1   2

1-2 MICA graduate students create a "meat suit treasure map" and make "trash kites" to engage kids and residents of East Baltimore.

like "Syphilis Biscuit" takes you. It might result in a clever program for staving off rural poverty (true story).

Of all the practices in this book, Let Go is the one that trips people up the most. That's why we often run several Let Go Drills back-to-back in quick succession to get people primed and loose. The good news is that the more you use Let Go, the more adroit you'll become at tricking your brain into a creative hyperdrive where unusual and surprising ideas emerge. Let Go quite literally changes your brain while seeding your future success.

Why Let Go?

Culturally, we are conditioned to be right from the moment we take a seat at a desk in a classroom. Teacher asks a question. Hands shoot in the air. The kids who know the right answer beam with pride. The kids who don't try to become invisible. Biologically, our brains form pathways to make us more efficient, but this can backfire. The goal of Let Go is twofold. First, it helps cancel out the heuristic and status quo biases by challenging you to make incredible, mind-bending associations. In doing this, Let Go invites you to consider problems in a fresh way.

The second goal is to generate as many ideas as possible without self-editing or needing to be right. Thinking right tells us to be confident in what we're suggesting before opening our mouths. It tells us to avoid looking foolish with some nutball idea. And it compels us to defend our thinking. An idea is presented, and we immediately start making a

1   2

Stop worrying about being *right*.

case for it being the right one. We dig in and stop being open to other potential solutions. You need to quell that desire to get immediate answers and, instead, imagine the vast possibilities. This is not the time for debate; this is the time to move quickly and think quantity over quality.

Our colleague Lance Rake, an industrial designer, likes to say that maybe 3% of ideas will survive; so if you generate 100 ideas, perhaps three will pan out. If you have only 10 ideas, well, you risk coming up empty. The more ideas you have, the more options. Think of it like cooking. There's a reality food show where contestants can win an advantage over competitors by getting more pantry items. The more ingredients, the more primed they are to create a stellar dish. The Let Go Practice helps you amass the largest set of possibilities for your solution, thus expanding the creative resources at your disposal.

The more you do this practice, the easier it becomes. The brain's plasticity means that it constantly rewires and re-routes its 100 trillion connections. "As long as you're learning anything new, you're forming new connections and probably dismantling other ones," Marc says. "You can definitely learn to let go, and it starts with an education that draws attention to the presence of these narratives."

So channel the spirit of the Syphilis Biscuit. Release a ton of wild, out-there, wacky ideas. We'll give you the tools to help you choose which ideas to explore further in subsequent chapters.

3   **4**

1 Random words connect the University of Notre Dame and South Bend. 2 World's largest living organism births a conference name. 3 Hacking a childhood favorite to sell Guidewire PolicyCenter. 4 "Okay, we're gonna take pictures of our clients' feet."

Getting Into the Let Go Mindset

It's time to imagine. Let Go is for the moment when you want to radically expand what might be possible. Thinking right pressures you to skip this step and jump to solving. The status quo wants you to have the answer, to be right, and to value efficiency over possibility.

The following drills will help you Let Go.

1   2

1 Aspirational spaces inspire Regus to be bold about the future of co-working. 2 The Love & Loathe Drill sparks ideas for healthcare delivery in Africa.

Be Uncensored.
Turn off your internal judge and let your ideas flow unfettered by what might be right or wrong.

Be Crazy.
Imagine the nuttiest, wildest, most outrageous solutions you can.

Be Prolific.
Put quantity before quality. You'll get to whittle things down later.

Random Word

Use when you need to let go of your problem-solving orthodoxies to generate convention-defying solutions.

Think Right
Start with what is already being done. Focus on improving or obsoleting that solution.

Think Wrong
Start solving from an entirely new place. Focus on generating as many possible solutions as you can from that new starting place.

For free Think Wrong Drill Resources go to:
www.thinkwrongbook.com/resources

What You Get
A shift in mindset from what is right to what is possible

A portfolio of unexpected, inconceivable solutions, ready for quick evaluation and further exploration

What You Need
Random Word Poster, Sharpies, Post-its, Blue tape, Brown paper bag

Instructions

Step 1 Introduce the Random Word Drill.

Step 2 Have teams place the two-word descriptions from the That's Odd Drill (see Get Out Drills) into a paper bag. Let each team choose two Post-its.

Step 3 Instruct Wrong Thinkers to use their random word pair as the starting place for generating ideas for how they might accomplish their moonshot.

Step 4 As they generate ideas, have them place Post-its on their Random Word Poster.

Tips Encourage Wrong Thinkers to begin with ideas that use all their words (e.g., Meat Suit Treasure Map). After a while suggest that they can use parts of words, or recombinations of letters in words, to further inspire their ideas.

Free associate.

Brand Takeover

Use when perceptions of what is—and is not— possible for your organization are holding you back.

Think Right
Let cultural conventions define what can and cannot be done.

Think Wrong
Hijack someone else's culture to imagine solutions that will "never fly here."

What You Get
Convention-bending ideas unbiased
by internal assumptions, orthodoxies,
and biases.

What You Need
Brand Takeover Poster, Brand
Board, Sharpies, Post-its,
Blue tape

Instructions

Step 1 Introduce the Brand Takeover Drill.

Step 2 Assign each team a brand from the Brand Takeover Tool
(available at www.thinkwrongbook.com/resources).

Step 3 Announce that the brand they've selected has taken over their organization. The good news: the new leadership thinks the work you're doing is vital.

Step 4 Have teams generate ideas for how their new brand owner might solve the challenge.

Step 5 Using Post-its, ask Wrong Thinkers to describe "The Bold Path"
(e.g., sustainable food supply, a clear connection between food and seed, real interest among the public, etc.).

Tips Prompt teams to use all assets associated with the brand that has taken over their organization. e.g., The Lego brand includes amusement parks, animated programming, characters, games, apps, educational products, discovery centers, and partnerships with major entertainment brands—in addition to their iconic plastic bricks. What might you do if you had those resources available?

Fake it.

MacGyver

Use when you want to make clever, practical, and original use of existing resources.

Think Right
Claim that a lack of time, people, and money stand in the way of innovation.

Think Wrong
Let constraints be a muse.

What You Get
Compelling hacks of existing resources and solutions that might prove easier to execute

What You Need
MacGyver Poster, Completed Asset Jam Poster, Sharpies, Post-its, Blue tape, Blindfold (optional)

Instructions

Run the Move Fast: Asset Jam Drill (see Chapter 6) before the MacGyver Drill.

Step 1 Introduce the MacGyver Drill.

Step 2 Have each team randomly choose three assets from their Asset Jam Poster.

Tips Be playful. Blindfold someone from each team before they pull their three assets in front of the group. Have them read aloud which assets they pull off the poster.

Step 3 Ask the group how many people know who MacGyver is. If there are people who do not know MacGyver from the TV show of the same name, introduce him.

Step 4 Inform Wrong Thinkers that, like MacGyver, they have limited resources and can use only the three assets to solve their challenge.

Step 5 Ask teams to come up with as many solutions as they can using only the three resources they have selected.

Escape the predictable.

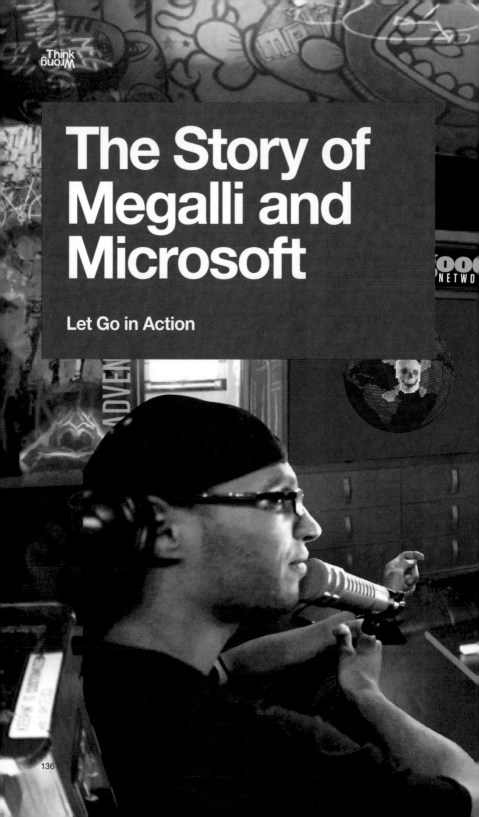

The Story of Megalli and Microsoft

Let Go in Action

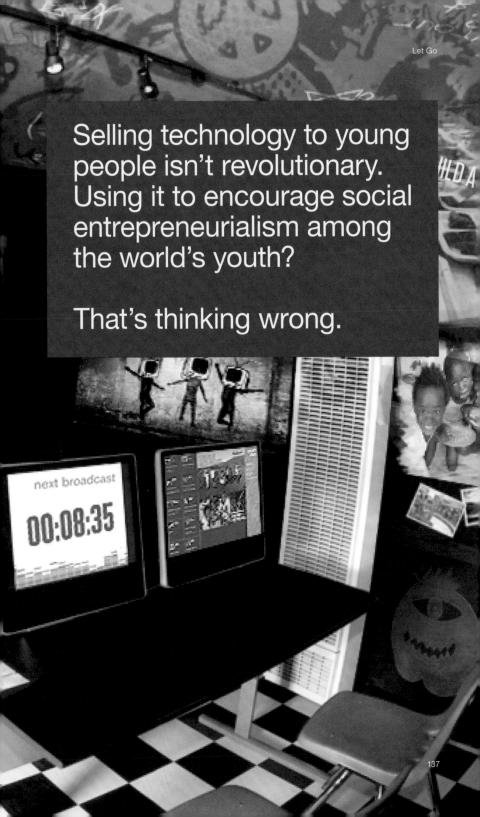

Selling technology to young people isn't revolutionary. Using it to encourage social entrepreneurialism among the world's youth?

That's thinking wrong.

Like neurologist Marc Diamond, brand strategist Michael Megalli understands the power of narratives. Michael is a renegade, the kind of guy who can peer years into the future and imagine what might exist for an organization or a business. Over his career he has worked with top global companies, and today he's using his creative dexterity to support entrepreneurs looking to change the world. Michael recognizes the power of storytelling in achieving that change. "The most interesting stories are the ones we tell ourselves," Michael says. "We have these internal narratives; it's the way our brains work. You tell yourself stories about your job, your family, your future—and these stories can be motivating, or they can be prison. We are constantly telling ourselves these stories that are incredibly powerful in directing our actions and ultimately the outcomes."

Michael is a natural Wrong Thinker, so we were stoked when he brought us in for a Think Wrong Blitz at Microsoft in 2012. Back then, Michael was senior director of brand strategy for the tech giant. He had been brought in specifically to act as a disruptive force from within. He knew from experience that overthrowing preexisting beliefs of what can and cannot happen within an organization is hard. Organizational narratives—the stories we tell ourselves about our companies—can be persuasive. And that's what was happening at Microsoft.

Microsoft had just launched a new billion-dollar initiative called YouthSpark, meant to give 300 million children across the globe access to education, life skills, entrepreneurial

We're throwing away the playbook.

opportunities, and technology. Part of the goal was to offer these kids a horizon shot—a glimpse of what their life and work might look like, should they harness the possibilities of education and entrepreneurship. Microsoft was ready to invest $500 million in cash and another $500 million in technology in 100 countries over three years to make YouthSpark happen. But what might that investment look like? How might it happen?

"A lot of the time, the corporate mindset was to go out and do customer research around a new idea," Michael says. "We come in armed with questions and the goal of interviewing people and getting to the bottom of this thing we want to understand. We had to get out of that normal pattern of doing things. That's what the Think Wrong Blitz was about."

We convened a group in Seattle for a two-day Blitz. We challenged the Microsoft team to go beyond merely introducing young people to technology and to think of how technology could be a vehicle for social change. If social enterprise is a driver of youth culture, how might Microsoft engage young people in this way? "The real focus in all of my work is around the idea of cultural relevance. This is very important for youth," Michael says. "Technology is just technology. Where it becomes powerful is in its application. It's not what we make, but what we make possible through that tech."

We introduced the practice of Let Go and asked the team to generate as many outlandish ideas as possible.

1　　　2

1 Michael Megalli's mission at Microsoft: Disrupt from within. 2 YouthSpark speaking to kids about YouthSpark? Crazy!

What crazy way might they get kids to connect life-altering ideas across the globe? Since Let Go is a generative practice, the goal was to throw as many ideas into the mix as possible, without editing.

Very quickly, we saw a problem. People were filtering their responses. They were self-editing based on existing notions of how things worked at Microsoft. The problem was clear: In an effort to generate ideas that might spark entrepreneurialism among the world's youth, the people in that room couldn't find their own entrepreneurial spark. They were stuck.

This is when we brought in a Let Go Drill known as Brand Takeover, which we share with you in this chapter. We broke the group into teams, gave each a different brand identity—Red Bull, the X Games, Virgin Atlantic— and said, "Now imagine that Microsoft has been bought, and YouthSpark is being run by this other brand."

Suddenly, the teams had energy. You could see the shift. Using another brand as a proxy sparked a host of off-the-wall ideas, from creating a clubhouse where kids could meet and exchange stories to the idea of a YouthSpark pirate radio station that would connect young people around the globe. When freed from their current corporate narrative, people let their imaginations run wild.

"That exercise that we did around Let Go was the key to the whole thing," Michael says. "People want to be given the freedom to get out of the organizational mindset. They want to hear: 'We're changing the rules. We're throwing away

Microsoft has been bought.

the playbook, and we're going to look at this problem in a way that's not encumbered by assumptions about the way it has always been done.'"

The trick, Michael says, is carrying the Let Go spirit back into your daily life. "How do you continue to think wrong after the Blitz is over?" he asks.

We understand. It's easy to fall back into old patterns. This is why Let Go is a practice that can—and should—be used anytime you feel stuck in your story. Pull a drill out during a weekly meeting to keep people energized. At Future, we use Let Go drills regularly to keep us honest, resourceful, and open to new concepts.

Michael left Microsoft in 2014 to launch indie.biz, where he's now creating a tribe of Wrong Thinkers by empowering entrepreneurs around the world to succeed in their quest for independent work.

The practice of Let Go is something he encourages in himself and in the clients, colleagues, and entrepreneurs he mentors. "If we want to create significant change—not just incremental change that improves our position a little, but significant change that makes the existing model obsolete—letting go is the key to the kingdom, so to speak. It creates a company culture capable of thriving and making a real difference."

1   2

1 Unlocking Microsoft's inner punk. 2 What would the X Games do?

4

Make Stuff

Green.

Picture that color. What do you see?

Maybe it's an azure-tinted green of the Caribbean ocean, or the saturated hue of a mountaintop tree line. Your green could be the oxidized tarnish of copper or the brightness of a lime. The point is we've got one simple word and myriad individual visualizations. What you see when we say "green" may be vastly different from what Mike sees, or Greg, or John. This is why paint chips exist, and why hairdressers show clients synthetic samples of dyed hair first. This is also why it's imperative in the development of a new concept to move from thinking to making.

There comes a point in any problem-solving process where talk becomes ineffectual. That first flush of excitement over tackling a challenge, and the adrenaline from generating lots of concepts, cedes to the stagnancy of so much banter. You've got all kinds of ideas, but they are just that: ideas. Mere suppositions. You could dispute these burgeoning ideas forever. Why it will work. Why it will fail. Who will support it. Who will kill it. Wait, what do you mean by GREEN?

This is a fool's errand. Without anything to test your ideas against, you're simply speculating. You're mired in debate and supposition, so progress halts. This is when it's time to start making.

Making stuff is how Andy Dreyfus, creative director at Pixar Animation Studios, and his team make Academy Award–winning movies such as *Finding Nemo* and *Toy Story*. On a recent visit to Pixar, Andy showed us the thousands

What do you mean by green?

green
green
green
green
green

of sketches and storyboards that went into making the film
Inside Out. When a team at Pixar conceives a story, they also
start to imagine what the characters and the scenery will
look like. The director, writers, and artists all have different
visions, so they start drawing. The early sketches are rapid-
fire, 30-second, freehand drawings. They aren't at all precise.
Some may be strange and abstract, yet they still communicate a concept that allows the rest of the team to see what
is inside a colleague's head. With each sketch, the team is
able to affix to things that work, rule out the things that don't,
and learn more about the characters in the story. The drawings get more detailed as they go along. Andy told us they
do this for the entire movie, and then they do it again. They
quite literally draw and conceive a film six or seven times
before it goes into animation.

You do not have to be as talented as the artists at Pixar
to flesh out ideas in this way. There's a famous scene in the
movie *Close Encounters of the Third Kind* where a young
Richard Dreyfuss sits at the kitchen table and madly sculpts
a tower out of mashed potatoes. His wife and kids watch in
horror as he transforms a side dish into an alien formation,
but he's a man with a vision, and there's no going back.
He needs to physically shape what he's seeing in his mind.

Make Stuff puts physical form to the ideas in your
head so you can understand them, share them, and quickly
evaluate them. Make Stuff is not about something pristine
or perfect. Far from it. It's about what comedian Chris Rock
calls "shitty first drafts." Sketches, a mocked-up logo, a

Sculpt something
out of mashed potatoes.

60-second video shot on your iPhone, a short scene acted out, a tagline. Draw with stick figures. Sculpt out of mashed potatoes. Suddenly the idea takes shape and it feels real. You can start to appreciate its potential.

The intention is a rapid and easy exploration of the challenge and solution, coupled with demonstrations that help the people around you envision it. With each iteration, you evolve the thing you're making. You create something new based on what you're seeing, learning, and hearing. When you make something, you discover what matters and what you can ignore. You generate deeper questions and more profound insights. You swiftly realize the idea had flaws, and you rule it out. We can't tell you how many times a person participating in a Blitz felt strongly about his or her idea, only to draw it and realize its limits. This is a good thing. You've just saved yourself a lot of time and energy heading down a short path.

In the world of design, Make Stuff is called rapid proto-typing. You're generating new ideas, just as you did in the Let Go Practice, but here you're using a different creative muscle. Something happens when you move from a thought to a thing. You understand the challenge and the opportunity more deeply through making, which leads to richer solutions. Milton Glaser, the artist and designer behind such iconic images as "I ♥ NY," points out that drawing *is* thinking. There's an invaluable mind-to-hand connection. When you sketch—or build, or sculpt, or craft—you trigger a new form of thinking (and, this hypothesis is backed by neuroscience: When

1   **2**

1 Starbucks Creative builds their making muscles by crafting Renga sculptures with Washington University's Bruce Lindsey. 2 Starbucks Blitzers enjoy the benefits of letting go of what they made.

children are prevented from drawing, their brains
don't develop fully.) Making, in other words, is essential
to understanding.

Why Make Stuff?
With Make Stuff, you move from high-level abstract thinking
to something more concrete. You move from Post-it notes
with a few scribbles on them and lots of verbal conjecture
to something explicit and detailed. If the practices we've
already discussed—Be Bold, Get Out, and Let Go—are the
lightning, then Make Stuff is your lightning rod. You start to
take the electric energy of your many ideas and ground them
in the tangible. It's not until you have something physical to
respond to that you really understand your problem and
your proposed solutions.

The goal of Make Stuff is experimentation and discovering what works and what doesn't through doing. This
practice derives from the same spirit as the scientific method.
Scientists frame a hypothesis, perform an experiment, and
make a discovery. If the experiment produces an unexpected
result, well, great! Now you know something you didn't know
before. You might even find that the unintended outcome
becomes the innovation. Electrical engineer John Hopp
meant to use radio frequency to treat hypothermia when
he discovered the pacemaker.

Ground your ideas
in the tangible.

Culturally, you have to fight the assumption that your initial hypothesis has to be right. Things not turning out as you expected is not failure; it's discovery. Biologically, you need to access the different parts of the brain that are engaged by the act of creating something tangible. Take a jazz musician, by way of example, and another scientific researcher named Charles Limb. Limb wanted to understand what happens inside the mind of a guy like John Coltrane when he improvised. So several years ago, Limb put musicians on their backs inside a functional MRI and gave them a customized keyboard to play. Limb discovered that activity in the area of the prefrontal cortex associated with self-monitoring declined, while activity in the prefrontal cortex area associated with self-expression went up. Players lost their inhibitions and became more creative in the act of making music. It's like Glaser's mind-to-hand connection— we engage new parts of our brain when we make, and this leads to both creativity and discovery. Enter the Make Stuff Practice—with the open-minded, investigative fascination that fuels a scientific researcher—and watch what happens.

1   **2**

1 Naming an early childhood development program makes it real. 2 A picture saves a thousand emails at Regus.

Getting Into the Make Stuff Mindset

This is the "Build" moment, when you move from verbal debate to making-based discovery. Make Stuff is still a generative process geared to learning. This process isn't about making the perfect, pristine, final THING; it's about experimenting in the real world and learning to evolve your solution. The Think Right approach to making and developing products or services is to be cloistered, proprietary, and secretive. It often involves big outlays of cash and resources to build from scratch, with the goal of launching with a market-ready solution. Think Right avoids sharing too early for fear of failure and/or theft.

The following drills will help you Make Stuff.

1   2

1 A German power company creates a beachhead into the American energy market. **2** The National Security Technology Accelerator imagines the Defense Innovation Network in a box.

Be Collaborative.
Find co-conspirators who have something unique to offer—including the people you are building with and for.

Be Ingenious.
Make clever, practical, and original use of existing resources when building your solution.

Be Simple.
Build just enough to answer your biggest questions— avoid overbuilding too early and be willing to share many shitty first drafts.

The Big Yes!

Use when you want to add new elements, experiences, and processes that might make your solution even more compelling, powerful, and real.

Think Right
Look for flaws and weaknesses in an idea—kill it before any exploration can occur (devil's advocate).

Think Wrong
Accept every offer, entertain any premise, build on ideas without limit or censorship.

What You Get
Deeper understanding of ideas

More robust concepts for ingenious solutions

New ideas

What You Need
The Big Yes! Posters (3 per team), Sharpies, Blue tape, Green dots

Instructions

Step 1 Introduce the The Big Yes! Drill.

Step 2 Have Wrong Thinkers select three ideas from their Let Go Drills and place them at the top of each The Big Yes! Poster.

Step 3 Ask one Wrong Thinker per team to start the drill. Have them write a "Yes And" Statement that elaborates on their selected idea.

When they've added their first Yes And Statement, have them move to the next poster.

Step 4 Have the next Wrong Thinker write a "Yes And" Statement, in response to the previous Wrong Thinker's "Yes And" Statement.

Tip Encourage Wrong Thinkers to top their teammate's contributions with even crazier, more far-out additions.

Step 5 Repeat Step 4 until each Wrong Thinker on the team has added a "Yes And" Statement to each of their team's ideas.

Step 6 Give each Wrong Thinker three green dots. Have them review all of the Big Yes! Posters, placing their dots on the "Yes And" Statements they find most compelling.

Say yes.

Name It

Use when you want
to craft a story for your
emerging solution—and
understand how people
might experience it.

Think Right
Rule ideas In or Out
before investing any
energy on them.

Think Wrong
Bring ideas to life to understand their potential—and
to allow them to inspire
other potential solutions.

What You Get
Better understanding of
your emerging solutions

Early use scenarios

Ability to share and
learn from others

What You Need
Name It Posters, Video camera,
Sharpies (black and colored),
Post-its, Blue tape

Instructions

Step 1 Introduce the Name It Drill.

Step 2 Have teams name their three emerging solutions.

Step 3 Ask teams to write a tagline for each solution.

Step 4 Have teams design a logo for each solution.

Step 5 Have teams illustrate key moments that reveal how their solutions might work.

Step 6 Have teams present their Name It Posters, reminding the group of the challenge or moonshot they are solving for—and for whom they are solving it.

Tips Name It is a good drill to record on video, so teams can engage others in their emerging solutions.

If time allows, and Wrong Thinkers have access to wi-fi, www.squarespace.com/logo is a nice tool to use to take their solution name and logo to the next level.

Sell it.

In a Box

Use when you want a clear, compelling, and concise presentation of your emerging solutions.

Think Right
Build a PowerPoint.

Think Wrong
Use an engaging form
to inspire your story rather
than forcing your story into
a business-as-usual format.

What You Get
Rough models of the product, services, processes, experiences, etc.

Clear and compelling language to describe your solution.

Who it is for. What it is best used for. How to use it. Reasons to believe in it.

What You Need
In a Box boxes, Video camera, Sharpies, Post-its, Blue tape, Colored markers, Glue gun, Foam core, X-ACTO knives, Play-Doh, Dowels, Printers, Ink, Paper, Photo paper, Flash drives

Instructions

Step 1 Introduce the In a Box Drill.

Step 2 Give each team three blank boxes.

Step 3 Allow individual Wrong Thinkers to choose which of the three ideas they want to work on (teams are welcome to work on all three).

Step 4 Instruct teams to bring their solutions to life using their boxes.

Top: Write a grabber that might make someone pay attention to the solution, plus a tagline.

Side 1: Describe what the solution is best used for.

Side 2: Describe who the solution is built for and the nature of the relationship between them and the provider of the solution (e.g., Athlete to Coach).

Side 3: Describe your solution's secret ingredients.

Side 4: Describe what the solution is guaranteed to do—and what its "OR" is (e.g., Guaranteed to make your smile brighter OR your money back.).

Bottom: Provide instructions or illustrate how to use the solution.

Step 5 Have teams present their boxes, reminding the group of the challenge or moonshot they are solving for.

Tips In a Box is a good drill to record on video, so teams can engage others in their emerging solutions.

Box it.

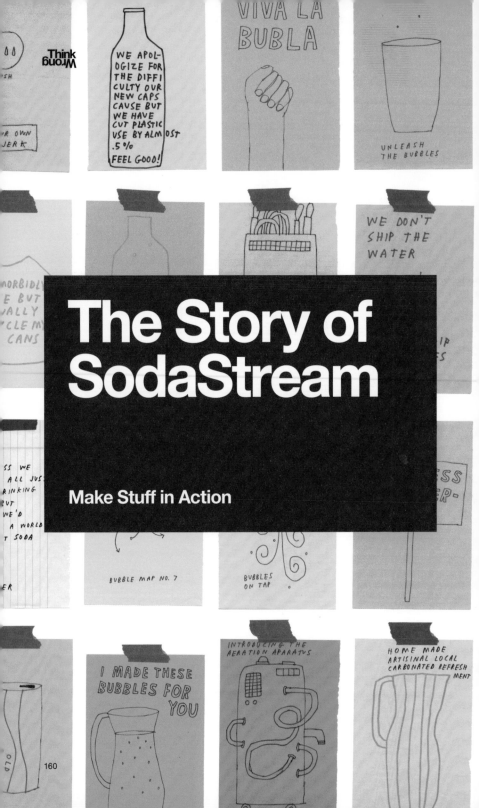

The Story of SodaStream

Make Stuff in Action

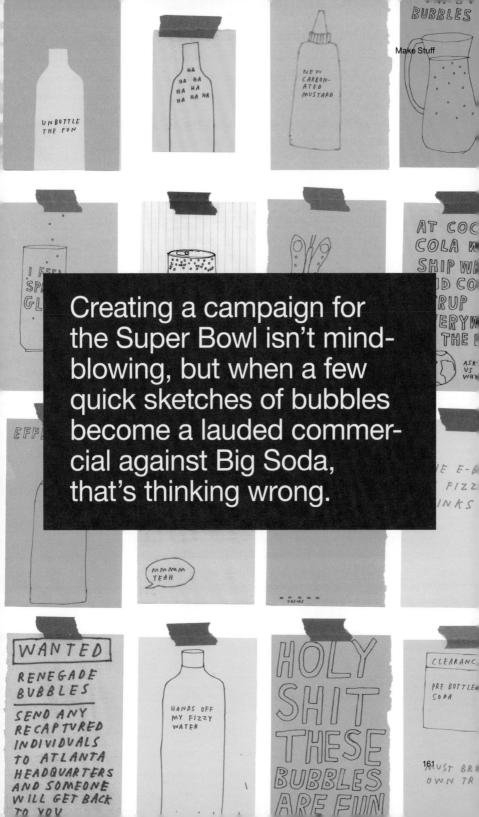

Creating a campaign for the Super Bowl isn't mind-blowing, but when a few quick sketches of bubbles become a lauded commercial against Big Soda, that's thinking wrong.

In 2013, an Israeli company called SodaStream became
a viral sensation when television broadcasters banned
its newest ad from playing during the Super Bowl.
SodaStream's countertop soda-making device uses com-
pressed air to add bubbles to tap water with the press of
a button. The unaired advertisement showed two delivery
men racing to bring palettes of Coke and Pepsi bottles to a
supermarket as dueling banjos play a frenetic tune. Suddenly
the plastic bottles explode in a burst of sugary water and cut
to a man using his at-home machine to make homemade
soda. "With SodaStream," the voiceover says, "we could've
saved five hundred million bottles on Game Day alone."

The commercial positioned SodaStream as the renegade, DIY soda of the future, and Big Soda as the relics
clogging landfills with so many single-use plastic bottles.
"If you love the bubbles," the voiceover says, "set them free."
The commercial may have been banned to run on television, but SodaStream aired it anyway via YouTube. Millions
watched, and everyone from *The New Yorker* to the
Huffington Post covered the story.

Flash back to a small studio in Boulder, Colorado,
in 2012, and you'll discover the genesis of this campaign
began with a tiny sketch of a bubble. It began with the
Make Stuff Practice.

1   2

It's fun. It's soda. It's bubbles.

We led a Blitz with SodaStream CEO Daniel Birnbaum and a few of his top execs at the FearLess Cottage, the studio of adman, activist, and designer Alex Bogusky. The goal was to discern how SodaStream might best position itself in the U.S. market.

We brought with us an Outsider, an artist named Tucker Nichols. Like Milton Glaser, Tucker thinks by drawing. His job was to sit back, observe, and make stuff. "I'm on the side at a little table with just a pair of scissors, markers, and a pile of paper," Tucker explains. "I listen to what's happening in the room, and I start drawing. At some point, I start tacking drawings to the wall. They start to self-organize, to show a story, and that can become meaningful."

At first, the talk in that room was serious business. The company aimed to make a dent in the market share of Big Soda. The practice of Making Stuff brought a necessary levity to the dialogue. "I have permission in the room that most people in those meetings don't have," Tucker says. "I'm drawing all the time; I'm working hard. People see what I'm making; they can see I'm not a jerk. But I tend to work in vague terms. I can usually get away with making fun of whatever we're talking about without offending everyone. At least most of the time. It's a courageous thing to bring someone in whose mindset right from the start is to try and figure out what's silly and present that back to the group."

3   **4**

1 The genesis of the "Free the Bubble" campaign was Nichols' sketch of a tiny bubble. 2 The Soda-Stream team wraps up three days of Thinking Wrong in Boulder. 3 Wrong Thinker Extraordinaire, Alex Bogusky's direct hit to Big Soda. 4 Designer Christian Helms takes bubbles to the streets.

The Make Stuff Practice contributed to the evolution of the ideas in that room. It gave SodaStream's top execs a tangible, physical thing to work against. "I remember John saying a bunch of times, 'This doesn't have to be so serious. It's fun. It's soda. It's bubbles.' And that got me thinking," says Tucker. He began sketching images of bubbles having fun. "The drawings started going more and more to the absurdity of bubbles," he recalls. "That's all soda is. Bubbles. We started playing around with that."

Tucker personified the bubbles, put them in crazy scenarios, imagined them freed from the constraints of Big Soda's plastic bottles. "I can't remember exactly where 'Free the Bubbles' came from, but that's where the conversation and the drawings went."

After the Blitz, SodaStream took the ideas born out of the Make Stuff Practice and made a Small Bet on an ad that could cause a sensation. (You'll learn more about Small Bets in the next chapter.) They Freed the Bubbles. And it worked.

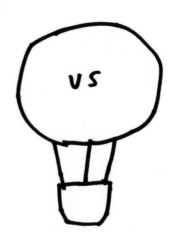

5

Bet Small

On a gusty October day in 2015, a 243-foot-long, helium-filled blimp broke loose from its mooring at a military base in Maryland and took a trip. The unmanned blimp, an experiment in military surveillance, had snapped its tether and was travelling at a decent clip while trailing 6,700 feet of thick cable. It crossed into Pennsylvania, where it took out power lines and startled a poor horse pulling an Amish buggy. Two F-16 fighter jets were dispatched to intercept the aerostat, while police warned people to stay inside and call 911 if they saw a 7,000-pound dirigible on the horizon. This blimp had gone AWOL.

Two decades ago, the U.S. military contended that a radar-equipped blimp would be a highly effective early-warning system against missile and drone attacks. Now, $2.7 billion later, defective software, erratic performance, and a tendency to crash in bad weather proved this was one investment gone awry. That this blimp took a meandering and destructive tour of the East Coast one week before Halloween seemed particularly fitting. The blimp is what defense insiders call a "zombie" program: expensive, ineffectual, and hard to kill.

The U.S. military may be known for its costly experiments and bloated bureaucracies, but zombie programs are not unique to them. Many of us throw good money after bad once we've made an investment in a new product or service or program or routine. We are too afraid to admit it's not working.

Expensive, ineffectual, and hard to kill.

There's a prevalent myth about innovation, and it's that bold and significant solutions require outsized risk. We bet the farm, gamble it all, and when it doesn't pan out, we're out of options. Conversely, we might never take the gamble in the first place. We fret over what we might lose—money, reputation, our job—so we sit on our hands and do nothing rather than risk failure. Well, it's time to put this myth to rest.

You can make significant change with reasonable small bets. In fact, Wrong Thinkers do this all the time. Our buddy Peter Sims wrote a book called *Little Bets,* and it showcases how some of the most creative talents in the world, from Steve Jobs to Frank Gehry, made continual, small bets to learn and grow. They didn't bet the whole farm. They bet a pony.

What if the U.S. military had said: *We don't know if this blimp idea is going to work. Remember the Hindenburg and all? Let's just place a small bet and see what happens.* A small bet might have presented some quick answers, like a windy day + balloons = problem, or an enormous white blimp makes one hell of an easy target when floating over enemy territory. It might have saved them 20 years, billions of dollars, and a heck of a lot of embarrassment.

Discovery is the goal— not being right.

Why Bet Small?

So here we are, at chapter five, and we've told you to be bold—to change how and where you get your inspiration, and who you collaborate with. We've had you generate lots of crazy ideas by letting go and making stuff. Now it's time to take that thing you've been developing and test it in the real world. How will it play with your intended audience?

When it's time to take an idea public, to test it in the marketplace, Wrong Thinkers are not binary. They don't believe that there is a right way and a wrong way and that the thing they are developing will either succeed or fail. Rather, they make a series of little experiments where *learning* becomes the key objective. They ask questions like: What is the thing we're trying to accomplish? What are our biggest questions? Where might we gain insights?

And once they glean those insights, they ask: Now what do we do with that learning and discovery? What's next?

The word "iterate" may be one of the most overused buzzwords these days and bordering on jargon, but we're here to argue its efficacy. Bet Small combats the binary "you're right" or "you're wrong" thinking that presumes you have to know all of the answers before going to market. Instead, you enter this phase with an inquisitive mind open to discovery, and you adjust as you go.

1   **2**

1 Genentech finds small ways to make a big difference in South San Francisco schools.
2 Charles River School discovers on-campus experience is the secret to recruiting new students.

Culturally, the status quo thinks in *right* versus *wrong* or *work* versus *didn't work*. Biologically, we don't invite change, big or small. We want to keep to what we already know. Bet Small is a framing device that alleviates the fear of looking stupid, and it stops you from doing nothing. It shifts the focus from ROI (Return on Investment) to LFI (Learn from Investment). And it allows you to keep learning. Discovery is the goal—not being right. You get quick clarification on your ideas and find that your inquisitiveness will be rewarded.

Getting Into the Bet Small Mindset

Bet Small helps you decide why, where, and when to invest your time and resources.

The following drills will help you Bet Small.

1   **2**

1 Not For Sale bets soup can free women from Amsterdam's Red Light District. **2** Secret Project students take thinking wrong on the road to build new relationships with the California College of the Arts.

Be Curious.
Let discovery drive
your solution.

Be Experimental.
Test your hypotheses and
treat unexpected results
as new opportunities for
breakthrough solutions.

Be Thrifty.
Use the least amount
of time and the fewest
resources possible to
get answers to your
most important questions.

LFI

Use when you place a higher value on discovering new things than on being right.

Think Right
Focus on ROI (Return on Investment) to create confidence or a reason to say "No."

Think Wrong
Focus on LFI (Learn From Investment) to learn more about the true nature of your challenge or opportunity, and what about your emerging solution works— and doesn't.

For free Think Wrong Drill Resources go to:
www.thinkwrongbook.com/resources

What You Get
Design, development, and
implementation priorities

Insight into the most fruitful small bets

Freedom from being right

What You Need
LFI Poster, Sharpies, Post-its,
Blue tape, Green dots

Instructions

Step 1 Introduce the LFI (Learn From Investment) Drill.

Step 2 Have Wrong Thinkers generate a set of questions raised by
their emerging solutions.

Step 3 Give three dots to each Wrong Thinker. Have them place dots
on the most challenging questions to address.

Optional Step Have Wrong Thinkers stack-rank questions,
with the first question to address at the top.

Be curious.

Do It On Monday

Use when you need insights to improve your solution.

Think Right
Execute large-scale solution.
Do nothing to avoid risk.
Blame others when things
don't turn out as predicted.

Think Wrong
Focus on the most important
questions raised by your solution. Design small bets to help
you learn the most with the
fewest resources.

For free Think Wrong Drill Resources go to:
www.thinkwrongbook.com/resources

What You Get
Clarity about which questions
need to be answered first

Portfolio of small bets

A low-risk path forward

Increased opportunity
for breakthrough insights

What You Need
Do It On Monday Poster,
Sharpies, Post-its, Blue tape

Instructions

Step 1 Introduce the Do It On Monday Drill.

Step 2 Instruct Wrong Thinkers to identify the three biggest questions
raised by their emerging solutions.

Step 3 For each of the questions selected, have Wrong Thinkers
identify what they might do on Monday using only three existing
resources, two colleagues, five days, and $50.

Step 4 Have Wrong Thinkers share their small bets with the group,
reminding the group of their emerging solution and challenging question.

Tips Small bets and affordable loss vary from group to group. Change
constraints to match what is "small" for the group you are working with.

Record each team on video while they share their small bets to help others
understand their immediate focus.

Tie your hands.

$100 VC Fund

Use when you want
to focus on what matters
most and what might
make the biggest difference.

Think Right
Defer to higher-ups
to dictate imperatives
and set priorities.

Think Wrong
Use the collective wisdom
of the group to determine
what has the highest
potential for impact and is
deserving of investment.

What You Get
Focus

Priorities

Alignment with what matters most

Insight into how teammates
think about priorities

What You Need
$100 VC Fund Poster, $100 in $1
bills, Video camera, Sharpies,
Post-its, Blue tape

Instructions

Step 1 Introduce the $100 VC Fund Drill.

Step 2 Instruct Wrong Thinkers to label the boxes on their $100 VC Fund Posters
with the names of the emerging solutions they are considering.

Step 3 Provide them with $100 in $1 bills.

Tip It's best to use real currency because people behave differently with real
money than they do with fake bills.

Step 4 Have Wrong Thinkers decide how they might invest their $100 fund
across the emerging solutions.

Step 5 Have teams explain why they allocated the $100 investment fund
as they did.

Tip Record each team's explanations on video to help others understand their
prioritization.

Place your bets.

The Story of Genentech

Bet Small in Action

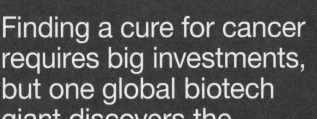

Finding a cure for cancer requires big investments, but one global biotech giant discovers the game-changing power of small interventions. That's thinking wrong.

The human immune system is a brilliant bit of biology. A foreign substance—bacteria, virus, parasite—enters the body, and our immune system kicks in, recognizing the offender and dispatching antigens to attack. Our bodies marshal resources to help protect us against disease.

Cancer, unfortunately, is equally as brilliant. It knows how to outsmart our natural defenses. Cancer cells manage to trick the immune system into ignoring their presence. *Nothing to see here!* they say. The cancer metastasizes unfettered and, well, you know what happens next. But what if there were a drug that could trigger our immune response to both see cancer cells and attack them? What if this molecule could shrink tumors? What if, in other words, we could outsmart cancer?

A few years ago, a scientist believed he'd discovered just such a molecule. Research into immunotherapy—using our body's immune system to combat chronic illness—has grown by leaps and bounds in the past few decades and great strides have been made in immunotherapy's use for cancer treatment. In his lab, the scientist saw promising results for a new drug capable of shrinking tumors.

Bench science is only the first step, however. Next, this molecule's efficacy had to be established in humans. In 2013, the biotech company Genentech tested this potentially life-extending medicine through a massive, global clinical trial. Running a clinical trial is both costly and complicated. Government and legal regulations require stringent protocols, and it is a slog getting a medicine safely to market. In this

People come and they get bored out of their minds.

case, the medicine showed such promising results that the team at Genentech was eager to get it vetted and out into the world. Genentech also faced incredible competition from other labs developing immunotherapy medicines. "The external forces pressuring the team were intense," says Kathryn Woody, who was operations program manager at Genentech at the time. "They needed to do something different and go at a faster speed by bringing the doctors and patients into the fold faster. All within constraints of regulatory and legal regulations."

The first step in any clinical trial is something called an investigator meeting. It's meant to educate the various clinicians—physicians, nurses, support staff—who will administer the investigational medicine to clinical trial patients via various healthcare institutions. It is also critically important to setting the stage for both the success of the trial and the quality of the patient experience.

Typically, participants in an investigator meeting gather in a city somewhere near the airport, where they spend hours at 60-inch round tables being talked at from a podium. You know that feeling when a lackluster presenter reads every word off every PowerPoint slide? Now imagine that *for days on end* and imagine it involves incredibly complex science. "People come and they get bored out of their minds," Kathryn says. "The protocols for running the drug trial, and the details about the science, are just being pushed at them. We'd used this same approach for the meeting over and over."

1   2

1 We asked, "What if we designed an experience we'd all want to have?" **2** Then we asked, "How might we tap into the emotional power of what we are doing together?"

Genentech hoped to kick off its clinical trial for a breakthrough medicine with a breakthrough investigator meeting. "This was a novel medicine, a novel concept, and we needed to move quickly," Kathryn says. "If we could do anything outside the status quo that was still within regulatory constraints, it was a no-brainer."

In the spring of 2013, Kathryn hired us to run a Think Wrong Blitz with the Genentech team. First, we brought in participants from across the organization—from executives to scientists to commercial and marketing teams. We included people who weren't generally invited to make decisions about clinical trial proceedings to help them let go of their modus operandi. "Usually companies do this sort of thing at an executive level, and then it trickles down, but this was a great way to get everyone involved," Kathryn says. "Once we were all gathered, Future did something interesting. They had us use only first names and no job titles to make sure everyone felt on equal ground." (We know from experience that diversity leads to better outcomes and that value comes from focusing on the meritocracy of the ideas versus the hierarchy of the people in the room.)

We spent the next two days imagining how Genentech might engage the doctors and nurses participating in investigator meetings more effectively. The elephant in the room—the big "Aha!" moment—was when the team reached a shared admission that these meetings can really suck for

They were on a journey to help outwit cancer.

everyone. The event had never been designed with an eye to creating value for the doctors, nurses, and administrators—and recognizing their valuable contribution to the development of a new treatment; rather, it was created to comply with governmental regulations. Out of that Blitz, Genentech decided to make a series of small bets to test the hypothesis that a better meeting would yield better results for everyone. They would flip the script on the typical event and host a more compelling meeting. They would tell the story of the medicine, the scientists who invented it, and the potential patients who might benefit from it, by using gripping narratives and design. This, in turn, would help the participants realize they were part of a bigger effort. They were on a journey to help outwit cancer.

We helped Genentech envision a portfolio of small bets that could make a big difference, and then we tried out the new strategy at an investigator meeting in Atlanta just two months later. Instead of using hotels near airports, the meeting was hosted at the Historic Academy of Medicine at Georgia Tech, a gathering center for the medical profession since 1941. An emcee helped keep the meeting running smoothly, and we coached the scientists to present the story of the medicine in a compelling way. We turned the protocols into a patient story by personifying who the patient might be and bringing the clinicians through that patient's treatment. The meeting was topped off by taking portraits of every

1　　　**2**

1 A real place, not a hotel ballroom. 2 Make the investigators, coordinators, monitors, and development team the heroes.

person who participated so Genentech could later acknowledge the many people who touched this medicine and helped to bring it from the bench to the bedside.

Genentech then quickly repeated these small bets at two more meetings across the globe. The effect was staggering. Surveys said this was the best investigator meeting these doctors and nurses had ever attended. "These simple changes made it clear that you're not just a cog in the wheel of this great grinding process; you're an integral part of one of the largest experiments in curing a fatal disease," Kathryn says. "You're a part of history."

1   **2**

1 Videos introduced the scientists behind the medicine. **2** Teach the protocol from the patient's point of view.

6

Move Fast

Think
Wrong

A few years ago, industrial designer Lance Rake fell off his bike. "Fell off," come to think of it, isn't exactly right. Lance fell *through* the bike. The whole frame, which he had designed, collapsed under his weight. He was pedaling along a flat expanse of pavement near his office at the University of Kansas, where he teaches design, and the bike began twisting underneath him like it was alive. Every pedal stroke and turn of the handlebars seemed an exaggerated demonstration of Newton's Third Law. The bike warbled, then cracked along the length of its down tube, and Lance tumbled to the ground.

This, believe it or not, was a good thing. Lance learned that the infrastructure he'd used to make the frame needed reinforcing. He dusted himself off and went back to his workshop to have another go.

Lance was attempting to design and build a sturdy, sustainable, easy-to-assemble bike frame out of renewable bamboo. Over his 40-year career, he had designed many things—from aircraft interiors to footwear—but never with bamboo. Then he heard about NADA bikes and the HERO-bike project in Greensboro, Alabama.

NADA began in 2009 on a hunch. It was the height of the fixie fascination—when bike messengers caused fixed-gear, single-speed bikes to spike in popularity—and John and a few cohorts wondered if the trend might be an opportunity to get young people in cities using bikes for everyday

He dusted himself off.

transportation. They made a small bet and bought 150 raw steel frames from Taiwan for about $60/pop. For $100, subscribers would get their NADA membership card—a bike frame—which they could accessorize as wanted, giving them a sense of ownership over their ride. The NADA team built a simple website and pushed the concept out through social media. Very quickly, the memberships sold out. They learned their instinct had been right.

NADA could have continued as first conceived, but it seemed strange to promote healthy living and sustainability while ordering steel frames from Taiwan. That's when the team got the idea to use bamboo. They consulted a small company in Brooklyn that was already making bikes out of the material. Meanwhile, down in Greensboro, Alabama, just 100 yards from where Project M had a studio, there was tons of the stuff. Could they use it? They cut some reeds, shipped them to the guys in Brooklyn, and learned their bamboo was Hearty Golden. Perfect for bikes. They developed a simple frame called the Gilligan, in honor of *Gilligan's Island,* and a Kickstarter campaign garnered $8,000 in pre-orders. HERObike was born.

When Lance visited the HERObike shop in the summer of 2011, he wondered if he could improve on the Gilligan design. "I was taking local Alabama bamboo and splitting it and sawing it and deplaning it and trying to bend it. I started making different kinds of tubes." Ultimately, Lance came up

1   2

The membership sold out.

with a hexagonal-shaped tube, inspired by memories of the bamboo fly rods his dad once used for fishing.

Lance returned to Kansas, where he researched, built, tested, and learned. The ride where he fell taught him that the tubes needed to be bigger, and they needed to be reinforced. "I got a relatively cheap lesson in frame design and understanding the difference between strength and stiffness," Lance says. "Bamboo is really strong. It is not stiff." He researched binding materials, then developed a braided carbon fiber sleeve to go inside the tube. A few months later, he had developed the elegantly simple and sturdy Semester Bike. "My process is to do a little bit of research, then build, find out what I don't know, and then research a bit more and build again," Lance says. "It's a lot of quick, iterative steps."

It's a process that his design students at Kansas struggle to embrace. "The tendency at first is to sit around and put a lot of Post-it notes on the wall. During presentations I always hear students say, 'This is a project to raise awareness,' and my response is, 'Don't raise awareness. Let's make something that actually works and do it in the field.' I challenge them to get deeper into a problem, and the best way to do that is to make as many things as quickly as possible and see what happens."

When experiments go south, like his bike ride, that's just part of the learning curve. It takes people time to get comfortable with that. "People like to think that they can

3   4

1 When you signed up for NADA, you received an unexpected membership card. 2 NADA bikes were cool. Shipping them from Taiwan was not. 3 Bamboo splits inspired the HexTube Carbon Fiber hybrid. 4 HERObikes quickly raised $44,000 to put the Semester Bike into production

make every step correctly on the way to a solution," Lance says. "We don't just want to get to the end; we want every step to be correct. But we have to throw that notion out and understand that the more steps we take, and the more mistakes we learn from, the more likely we are to get to a successful end. Keep making steps, keep moving quickly, and learn to reassess from where we are, rather than looking too far ahead or too far back."

In three short years, the concept of encouraging an urban biking community moved from 150 steel frames made in Taiwan to a sustainable business in Greensboro that inspires people to ride, all while revolutionizing the design of bamboo bikes. Lance has since become a specialist in the material and is building everything from bikes to skateboards and paddleboards out of bamboo.

Why Move Fast?
The Move Fast Practice is the antidote to getting bogged down. When problems arise, it's easy to get derailed. Our human biology is to avoid decisions that might carry risk and to procrastinate by kicking the proverbial can down the road. At work we see this tendency materialize in an endless cycle of email chains and in calling for yet another meeting. We conduct more research and give something its "due diligence." It's the circuitous workplace ouroboros. We just keep going in circles. Our cultural predisposition favors rigid job titles and the politics of posture: We often want to be

Bias to action over dissection of direction.

right and to do things the way we think best. How often has a really good idea made its way up the chain of command, only to get killed because the person at the top prefers the way he or she thinks it ought to be done? Too often, we thwart fast action because we'd rather have an outcome we perceive to be politically advantageous to us. This leads to procrastination, which creates a progress-killing vacuum.

Move Fast is all about becoming friends with the unknown in order to test a host of possibilities quickly and to expedite results that matter. It represents a bias to action over dissection of direction.

"Whenever you're trying to come up with a new way of doing something, a big part of what you have to do is think of many different ways to do it, and most of those ways aren't going to work," Lance says. "You must have a way to go through a lot of ideas that don't work, and you have to do it quickly."

The Move Fast Practice was designed to build the momentum necessary to plow through uncertainty, mistakes, and confusion to reach results. (Or as some Blitzers from the Navy explained to us: "JFDI"—Just F&*%ing Do It!)

1   **2**

1 Rita McGrath and Linda Yates of mach49 riff on managing change inside a corporate mothership.
2 Major pet food brand thinks wrong about their business, launching a start-up in two days.

Getting Into the Move Fast Mindset

Move Fast accelerates the learning process so you can push your difference-making solutions out into the world. Small bets build momentum, reach, and sustainability of solutions.

The following drills will help you Move Fast.

1   **2**

1 Roche, governments, universities, and caregivers think wrong about healthcare delivery across Sub-Saharan Africa. **2** Leaders think wrong at the White House to transform political engagement among Asian Americans.

Be Open.
Share broadly across your team, organization, communities, industries, regions, and nations, and be humble enough to listen to others' points of view.

Be Confident.
Accept uncertainty and incomplete knowledge; embrace that you know enough to progress.

Be United.
Integrate learning from across your portfolio of small bets to build momentum, reach, and sustainability of solutions.

Asset Jam

Use when you want to make the most out of resources already available to you.

Think Right
Prepare business case
for large-scale investment.

Think Wrong
Let resource constraints
inspire ingenious solutions
to your challenge.

For free Think Wrong Drill Resources go to:
www.thinkwrongbook.com/resources

What You Get
Inventory of resources
with which to solve

Recognition that there
is much to work with

What You Need
Asset Jam Poster, Sharpies,
Post-its, Blue tape, Butcher paper
(optional)

Instructions

Step 1 Introduce the Asset Jam Drill.

Step 2 Have Wrong Thinkers place their new challenge, moonshot, or emerging solution (depending on your focus) at the center of their Asset Jam Poster.

Step 3 Have teams use Post-its to identify the resources available to solve with.

Optional Step Use two colors of Post-its to distinguish between currently available resources and additional resources that might be required.

Optional Step *The Big Jam:* Have teams rotate to the team location to their right. Ask one Wrong Thinker per team to stay behind to explain their challenge or moonshot to other teams as they rotate through and build on assets. Rotate teams every 60 seconds until they are back to their team home.

Tip Asset Jam can also be run as a group drill. We have used large sheets of butcher paper to create a giant Asset Jam Poster by hand.

Take stock.

Impact x Doability

Use when you need to prioritize ideas for impact.

Think Right
Conduct time-consuming
and expensive research
and analysis of ideas—
looking for case studies,
best practices, and data
to support ideas.

Think Wrong
Use the collective wisdom
of the team to rapidly sort,
evaluate, and select the
most compelling and
highest-potential ideas.

What You Get
Definition of high impact

Definition of what makes a
solution easy or difficult to execute

Prioritization of ideas for
further development

What You Need
Large empty floor or wall space,
Post-its, Blue tape

Instructions

Step 1 Introduce the Impact x Doability Drill.

Step 2 Use blue tape to create a large L-shaped space on the floor or wall.

Label the vertical axis "Impact" with "Very Little" at the bottom-most point
and "Extraordinary" at the top-most point.

Label the horizontal axis "Doability" with "Nearly Impossible" at left-most
point and "So Easy" at the right-most point.

Step 3 Have Wrong Thinkers use Post-its to describe "Impact," placing
them to the left of of the vertical "Impact" axis.

Step 4 Have Wrong Thinkers use Post-its to describe "Doability," placing
them below the horizontal "Doability" axis.

Step 5 Instruct Wrong Thinkers to position the ideas generated from the
Let Go Drills in the "Impact x Doability" space—with everyone placing ideas
at the same time.

Step 6 Ask Wrong Thinkers to select the three, high-impact ideas their
team is most excited about developing further.

Tip Encourage all Wrong Thinkers to participate in placing the ideas rather
than telling one or two teammates where the ideas ought to be placed in
the "Impact x Doability" space. If there is a disagreement with placement,
move it, and discuss why you moved it with the group.

Prioritize it.

SASU

When you want to learn from others about how your solution might make even more of a difference.

Think Right
Present and defend.

Think Wrong
Share and shut up (SASU) so that you can really hear the feedback.

What You Get
Valuable feedback from peers

Practice active listening

What You Need
Video camera, Pens, Notebooks

Instructions

Step 1 Introduce the SASU Drill.

Step 2 Instruct teams to present their solutions in the allotted time and to listen to feedback without responding. Encourage each team to appoint a note taker.

Step 3 Have each team present while timing each presentation.

Step 4 As a group, discuss how the team might depart even further from the status quo:

What stands out and apart from known solutions?

Where are there opportunities to depart even further?

What trends, technologies, or assets might create greater separation from the predictable path?

What questions are raised by the solution that has been presented?

Tip Set a time limit for both presentations and feedback. SASU is a good drill to record on video so teams can engage others in their emerging solutions.

Listen up.

The Story
of dmgi

Move Fast in Action

Wanting your people
to be more innovative
isn't revolutionary.
Disrupting your business
from the inside out?

That's thinking wrong.

The Silo. That great architectural symbol of isolation. In today's corporate-speak, "breaking down silos" is perhaps one of the most common of mantras. Move outside your encapsulated department or discipline. Disrupt business as usual. Cross-pollinate in order to accelerate change. Aiming a wrecking ball at a metaphorical silo is a nice concept, but what does this mean in practice? Take a long walk down the hall from one department to another, present a daring idea to the CEO, to the board of directors, to your strategic partners, and watch as the walls quickly rebuild. Breaking down silos translates, in actuality, as a willingness to risk new ways of doing business, and that's where people get stuck.

"The problem is that, in many companies, when you want to do something new, you have to follow an existing process that doesn't allow for risk," says Eric Frank, a global business strategist at dmg::information (dmgi), a division of the Daily Mail and General Trust plc (DMGT), a UK-based multinational portfolio of information businesses and media brands. "You have to draft a plan and make a financial model and argue for your idea's efficacy. You have to get buy-in first, and then you have to deliver on what you've already promised."

Eric notes that when a Silicon Valley VC funds a start-up, "If you blow up, you blow up. You're expected to test out new ideas, fail quickly, get back on your feet, and keep on doing that until you've figured this new thing out. Traditionally that's been tough to do inside most companies unless someone

Be willing to risk new ways of doing business.

from above says, 'It's OK, I'm going to back your risk'—
and at dmgi, we have that."

Today many companies are setting up satellite offices
in Silicon Valley. They hope that through osmosis something
big might happen. Linda Yates knows from experience that
creating a new and viable venture, and doing it quickly, is
about more than mere geography. For 30 years, Linda has
been a bridge between the Silicon Valley and large corpora-
tions. In 2013, she co-founded mach49 to help Global 1000
companies incubate and accelerate new opportunities by
bringing teams of people to the Valley and connecting them
with the talent and processes that fuel innovation. We partner
with mach49 to teach these companies to think wrong.

dmgi and its parent company DMGT had a long tradition
of diversification and innovation during its 120-year history,
but in 2015, its leaders realized they needed to learn how to
innovate in a new way. The company turned to mach49.
dmgi invests in and manages business-to-business information companies, and over the years it had acquired a number
of firms that were specializing in real estate information.
"We needed some way to generate ideas internally rather
than buying new businesses," Eric says. "We decided to
make an investment and use our commercial real estate
companies as the proxies."

The challenge, Eric explains, is that dmgi had a
silo problem.

"In the U.S. we have six different real estate companies
working independently of each other. We have assets in

1   **2**

1 dmgi leaders took ownership of the new business
idea through shared authorship of it. 2 Speed to
solutions is increased by removing time for debate.

these companies. So how do we not only get internal innovation, but also cross-company collaboration? How do we leverage what we have?"

During a two-day Think Wrong Blitz in Soho, New York, we helped the CEOs and employees of these companies quickly see the potential of what already existed. "We needed to get out of our normal routine, get our companies collaborating with each other, and force them into a room to talk about common threads," Eric explains. "But we also wanted to engage them in a process of thinking differently about their work. Could we find a good idea or two to pursue, and could we also get people to internalize this process and bring it back to their own companies?

"The Blitz got us to think differently about product development and collaboration. We learned how to think about opportunities and the assets that we already had, and then how we might leverage that into something new."

One of the assets these companies had was a vast network of data on commercial buildings. How might they turn this information into something of value to a consumer?

That question spurred a few ideas, including one for a business that acts like a mash-up of Zillow and OkCupid for commercial real estate. "The question then became how do you take that idea and work with customers, work in an accelerated fashion, and turn it into something that you could quickly adapt, test, and realize?" Eric says.

A team of eight people was selected to go for three months to develop and validate the desirability, feasibility,

This was not about creating a new silo.

and viability of this new business hypothesis at the mach49 incubator in Silicon Valley. Once there, they were given the training, coaching, and resources necessary to experiment and quickly learn if the idea was worth pursuing.

The incubator team did not—and this is key—work in isolation. This was not about creating a new silo, where a small group emerged at the end excited by a concept only to shock or confuse company decision-makers. Instead, the team reported back to the organization—the "mothership" as we call it—on a regular basis. "We kept the CEOs in the loop to see that it didn't end with just a good idea," Eric says.

The team developed a concept for a new commercial real estate search engine and rating service, including a mobile app, that would help users match their needs to the perfect commercial space. At the end of the three months, the business was presented to dmgi, and the decision was made to fund the new venture. In a few short months, the company went from a collection of companies unsure of how they might work together, to collaborating on the creation of a viable and exciting new business called Spaceful.

Equally as important, Eric says, is what the individuals learned about how to approach work. "Those who went into the incubator are now our internal evangelists. We hope that we can scale their experience to the daily practice of people across all our companies."

1   **2**

1 Time limits inspired collaboration rather than pontification. **2** This Blitz produced eight 90-second business pitches. One placed into the mach49 incubator. One inspired new business acquisition. One improved current operations of existing dmgi business.

TW

Another breakthrough idea smacks down the way things are.

a
c
k
!

Another bold step forward.

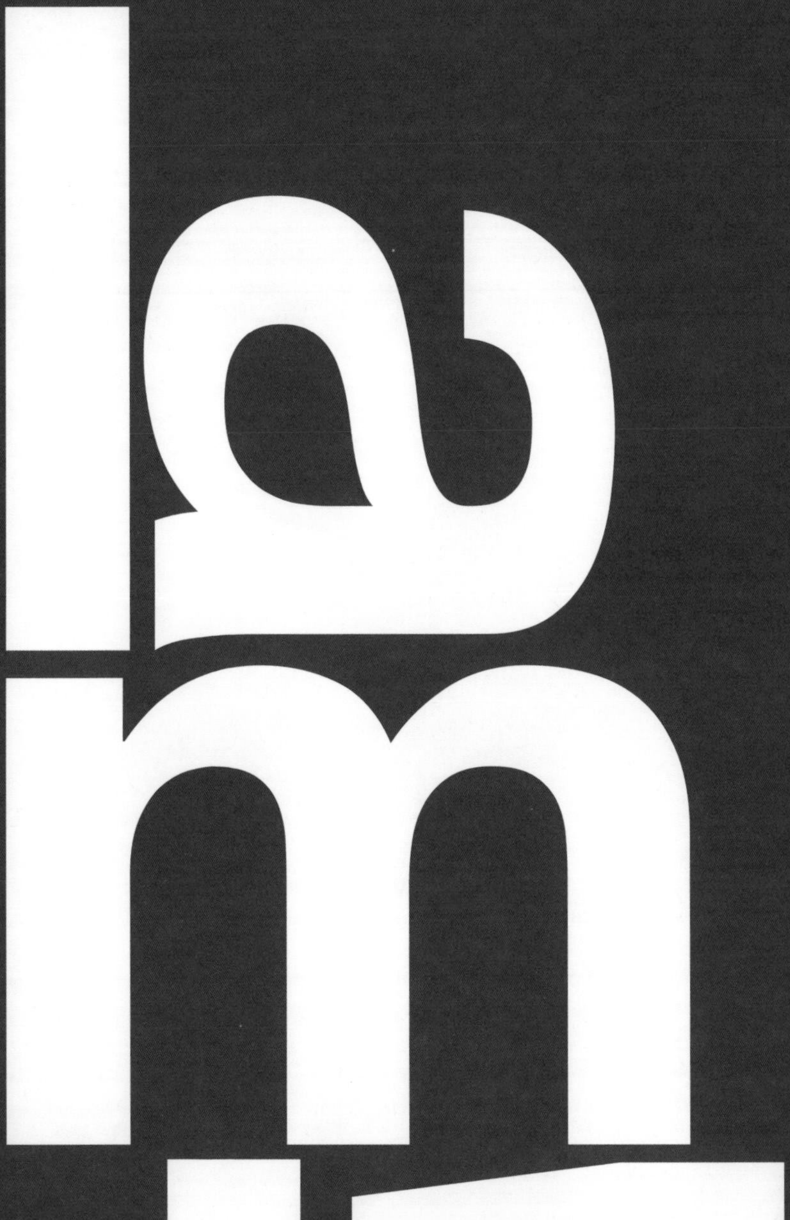

A stiff uppercut
for progress.

W!

The door to a better
tomorrow slams open.

We know you're ready to change the way things are.

You're excited about something, an idea or a new solution with real potential.

You share the epiphany with your boss, your board, your colleagues, your investors, your friends.

And this happens.

HOLY

I can't
believe it!

This
just
might
work!

Let's make it weirder!

Yes, and...

Your opportunity to do work that matters takes flight.

Welcome to the Think Wrong Club.

For us, this work is personal. We have children who will inherit the most wicked and stubbornly resistant problems that conventional right-thinking problem solving has inadvertently caused, failed to find, or stymied the answers to. If our kids' generation is to have any hope of resolving the unprecedented challenges facing mankind, we must help more people move off the well-worn paths that have gotten us to this place—we need a new problem-solving system.

None of us can do this alone. If we really want to make a difference, we realized, then it's a matter of scale. We could try to do this work as three partners at a firm. Or we could teach teams of people to think wrong and unleash their ingenuity on the world. Our mission at Future is to drive positive change, and, for us, the best way to do that is to empower as many people as possible to think wrong. We want to give you the necessary resources to bring crazy, mind-bending, seemingly magical, world-changing solutions to life that conventional methodologies could never find. We want to foster resilient, resourceful people capable of making a difference and blazing bold new paths.

The founding members of the Think Wrong Club featured in this book have two things in common.

First, they are deeply driven to make a difference. They are cultural outlaws who are happiest operating outside the bounds of convention. They cannot help but see things both as they are and as they should be.

Second, they share a frustration with how difficult and slow it is to create the change they envision. Each unsatisfying encounter with the status quo within their organization, community, political body, academic institution, or government makes them want to pound their head against the wall.

We also see that their conviction, determination, and persistence alone are not enough to escape the status quo, or those hell-bent to protect it. Thinking right already has its language and its tools; it's already got its best practices, defenses, and case studies. In the think-right world of brainstorming, focus groups, marketing surveys, number crunching, bottom lines, and ROI-focused agendas, it's hard to defend something nebulous and new. Wrong thinkers need their own language, frameworks, tools, and techniques to counter the existing norms.

We're not alone in filling this void—Wrong Thinkers such as Warren Berger, Steve Blank, Tim Brown, David and Tom Kelley, Bruce Mau, Rita McGrath, Alex Osterwalder, Eric Reis, and Louis Rosenberg are changing the way big gnarly problems are solved in business, government, education, civil society, and beyond.

This book is our attempt to arm you—and people everywhere—so you may conceive the inconceivable and bring the Shepherds, Scouts, Sheriffs, and Posses in your organization along with you to implement, scale, and operate your status quo–busting solutions. It's a toolkit to accomplish your ambitions.

We hope you use it to identify the biological and cultural hurdles that stand in your way at critical moments. To adopt a mindset that you can apply to counter the status quo. To put the Think Wrong Practices into action. To dream, seek, imagine, build, learn, and share—free from the confines of business as usual and the strongly held assumptions of the way the world works that no longer hold true.

We hope you will come to master the Think Wrong Practices, Mindsets, and Drills. Like training for a marathon, with each run, you go a little farther, you run a little faster. Many of our clients have become so adept at thinking wrong that they've developed their own drills tailored to their unique needs. We anticipate you will be able to do the same. Once embedded, thinking wrong won't just change the outcome of individual tasks and initiatives. It will become your way of operating in the world—exploring, discovering, and imagining new possibilities—while staying outside the reach of the status quo.

Don't be surprised if it changes not just how you work, but the way you live. Notice how the ethos of Be Bold, Get Out, Let Go, Make Stuff, Bet Small, and Move Fast filters into your daily life, propelling you to rethink your quotidian routine.

As you begin your think wrong adventure, remember one important thing: Suspend disbelief. Imagine if, seven years ago, John had piped up and said, "This pie idea? Bonkers."

John knew better than to kill that nascent idea.

He understood a fundamental truth we have all come to appreciate after years of experience: The seemingly crazy notions are the ones that change everything. You just have to be open to them—and equipped to protect them—while you shape and grow something incredible. The status quo will take a swipe at you 100 times a day. Now you're ready to land a counterpunch. So the next time biology and culture try to force you back onto the predictable path, don't just resist. Swing back. Think wrong.

—John, Mike, and Greg

Acknowledgments

If it were not for some incredibly talented wrong-thinking individuals, generous in both time and spirit, you would not be reading this book—probably out of choice, as it would have been a droning, hideous tome.

Thanks goes to all of those who appear in the book for sharing their stories, and to their organizations for allowing us to share them with the world.

Special thanks needs to be given to a few who shaped this book immensely.

Elizabeth Evitts Dickinson, a virtuoso storyteller. She spent countless hours listening to us debate, quibble, vacillate, and pivot. She prodded and steered us, and then somehow channeled our minds, voices, and spirit to extract the nuance of our intentions. She crafted words people would want to read—all while maintaining patience, humor, and all-around affability (no wonder rock stars hired you to go out on tour). Simply put, there would be no *Think Wrong* without her.

Michael Braley, a quiet master of design. He created a book we couldn't have imagined—never mind realized. His design elevates thinking wrong in ways only an artist could. Thanks for your steely determination and meticulous attention to details— we, our readers, and future Wrong Thinkers are in your debt.

Lily Piel, *Think Wrong's* eyeball. Her artistry and empathy captured the experience of thinking wrong. Her photos bring to life the intensity, fun, and soul of the Blitz experience and our merry band of Outlaws fighting the good fight against the way things are.

Chris Conroy, Gilles Frydman, Victor Penner, and Sarah Thorpe, equally amazing talents behind the camera whom we endorse and cannot recommend highly enough. Thank you for bringing your passion, spirit, and talent to this strange thing that we do.

Becky Schultz, the engine that could—and does. Thank you for searching, sorting, scanning, and making sense of our many unclear, contradictory, and confusing requests in such good humor. You bring joy to our collaboration that not only makes what we do better, but makes our lives better. Thanks for being the amazing human that you are.

And the dearest for last. We thank our families who put up with us day in and day out as we strive to walk the bold path and say no to the status quo. Your encouragement, support, and willingness to stand by our sides as we repeatedly step into the unknown make it possible. We love you all (there it is in black and white).

Index

Footer photos and captions are
indicated by f following the page number;
multiple footer photos and captions are
indicated by ff.

Let's get started.

Rita's Think Wrong Cheat Sheet

Columbia Business School professor, and one of the world's leading experts on strategy in highly uncertain and volatile environments, Rita Gunther McGrath sketched out this cheat sheet to help you get ready to think wrong.

Conditions for Think Wrong Success

When completing your checklist, stack the cards in favor of your success.

Framing Your Think Wrong Challenge

Use this outline to get started on framing your challenge.

Your Quick & Dirty Checklist

☐ Frame your challenge.

☐ Invite the mix of minds you want in the room (your content experts, functional experts, lateral thinkers, makers, and so on).

☐ Identify where you will think wrong.

☐ Select—or invent—the drills you will use.

☐ Engage your Wrong Thinkers in a high swarm of idea generation, making, and ranking.

☐ Generate a portfolio of potential solutions—avoid trying to come up with *the* solution.

☐ Have an action plan for the emerging solutions and small bets you will generate.

How might we:

(what you want to accomplish),

For:

(whom your impact will matter most to),

In a way that:

(describe the approach, mindset, or values you want to apply),

So that:

(the big impact you want to create).

Think Right

Convergent, narrow problem statements

Small, intact teams who work together a lot

"Relevant" expertise and experience emphasized

Conference rooms and hotel meeting spaces

Slow, tidy, and deliberate

Focus on research, text, analysis, and best practices

Safe and predictable

Analyze, debate, win, lose

Value being right and risk avoidance

Textual and verbal output

Incremental adaptation of what exists and has been proven

Large program spends

Modest impact goals

Think Wrong

Divergent, broad
problem statements

Large, diverse teams
who are often strangers

Diverse perspectives, experiences,
and knowledge emphasized

Unusual, unexpected,
provocative spaces

Fast, messy, and deliberate

Focus on inspiration, imagery,
imagination, and ingenuity

Surprising and disorienting

Generate, collaborate, co-create

Value great questions
and experimentation

Visual and tangible output

Entirely new solutions
without regard for what is

Small, focused spends

Massive impact goals

Think
Wrong

Think
Wrong
Resources

Introductory Video Clips

Short video clips show you when to use the drills featured in *Think Wrong,* describe how best to introduce them, and offer tips on executing them with your team.

Think Wrong Drill Tools

Want to help others think wrong? Using Future's cloud-based Think Wrong Lab, create your own Think Wrong Challenge Poster, download Think Wrong Drill Posters, and access the Brand Takeover Tool.

You want to drive positive change. You're creative, passionate, and committed to making things better. Authors John Bielenberg, Mike Burn, and Greg Galle provide you with access to free online resources to help run the 18 drills featured in *Think Wrong*. These tools will help you put the book's ideas into action.

Visit www.thinkwrongbook.com/resources to access your free resources.

Think Wrong Blitz Task Manager
Plan how to design, produce, and run your own Think Wrong Blitz— and how to follow up on what you produce—using this handy to-do list based on the Think Wrong Lab's interactive planning tool.

Think Wrong Shop
Don't waste time hunting for supplies. Use Future's Think Wrong Shop to purchase materials you'll need to run the drills featured in *Think Wrong*.

Flex your inner Wrong Thinker.

Use our cloud-based Think Wrong Lab to create status–quo busting solutions to any challenge—big or small.

Let thinking wrong become how you operate in the world.

The Think Wrong Lab provides individuals, teams, and organizations with access to the language, frameworks, tools, tips, and techniques necessary to explore, discover, and imagine new possibilities, conquer the status quo, and do work that matters.

www.thinkwrong.com/member

"With the Think Wrong Lab
you can design, like a benevolent
genius, a status quo–obliterating
working session for any challenge
you can imagine. Try it, I dare you."

Adam Butler, founder and
Strategic Chief, The Butler Bros

About the Authors

John Bielenberg, Mike Burn, and Greg Galle
work together at the Silicon Valley innovation products and
services company Future Partners. Along with the Future
team they provide cultural outlaws, frustrated by their
attempts to jailbreak the status quo, with the language,
frameworks, tools, and techniques they need to escape
biological and cultural forces so they can drive positive
change in their organizations, communities, countries, and
the world. They build software, train and coach leaders and
teams, run immersive workshops, and partner with creative
firms around the world to help them do work that matters—
and makes a difference.

Elizabeth Evitts Dickinson is an award-winning journalist
and editor who writes about architecture, design, culture,
and creativity.

Book Design: Michael Braley
Photography: Chris Conroy,
Gilles Frydman, Victor Penner,
Lily Piel, Sarah Thorpe
Copy Editor: Darcy Kendall,
Kristen Pinheiro
Index: Maria Sosnowski
Printer: Blanchette Press